STRATEGIES for
RURAL
COMPETITIVENESS:

Policy Options for State Governments

By Thomas W. Bonnett

C | G | P | A

COUNCIL OF GOVERNORS' POLICY ADVISORS

Library of Congress Cataloging-in-Publication Data

Bonnett, Thomas W., 1952 -
    Strategies for rural competitiveness : policy options for state
    governments/ Thomas W. Bonnett.
        p.   cm.
    Includes bibliographical references and index.
    ISBN 0-934842-71-X
    1. Rural development–United States. 2. United States –Rural conditions. I. Title.
    HN90.C6B66 1993
    307. 1 ́412 ́0973 – dc20   93 -11723
                                                                        CIP

Cover design by Hasten Design Studio, Inc.

Printed in the United States of America.

The Council of Governors' Policy Advisors is a membership organization of the policy and
planning staff of the nation's governors. Through its office in Washington, D.C., the Council
provides assistance to states on a broad spectrum of policy matters. The Council also conducts
policy and technical research on both state and national issues. The Council has been affiliated
with the National Governors' Association since 1975.

Council of Governors' Policy Advisors
400 North Capitol Street
Suite 390
Washington, D.C. 20001
(202) 624-5386

Alice Tetelman, Executive Director

**This project was supported by the Aspen Institute, the Ford Foundation, and the
W.K. Kellogg Foundation.**

CONTENTS

LIST OF BOXES AND CHARTS

ACKNOWLEDGMENTS

In 1974 I was very fortunate to be elected to the Vermont House of Representatives. My principal concerns were education and environmental protection. Near the end of this first term, the severity of the national recession shifted my attention toward efforts to create more jobs for the residents of the four small towns that I represented. This was a challenge — what should state government do to enhance job creation? What could this rural community do to promote economic development?

Several aspects of this personal challenge come vividly to mind: the lack of practical information about economic development strategies that might be appropriate for my rural community; the intensity of the jobs versus environment trade-off, which was referred to, inaccurately, I thought, as the "six-packers versus the back-packers"; and the frustration of attempting to explain a policy position on economic development that I realized was intellectually weak.

I was not alone in acknowledging the weakness of my position. An editorial in the local daily newspaper tweaked my feeble suggestion that we could recruit "clean, light industry to the area." The editorial simply asked why clean, light industry would be interested in locating there. Naturally, I had no good answer.

Nevertheless, I was reelected in 1976, and I spent much of my second term trying to understand economic development policies and programs. I was searching for a good answer to what state government could and should do to nurture more business and employment opportunities in rural communities. I have since continued this search, and this book is an attempt to present a more thoughtful response to the questions I first encountered almost twenty years ago. I am grateful to have had this opportunity. So, it seems appropriate that the first person I want to acknowledge and thank is that editorial writer who in 1976 challenged my political bunkum.

I want to thank my current and former colleagues at CGPA: Michael Campbell, Judith Chynoweth, Lauren Cook, Barbara Dyer, Leslie Fain, Tony Hutchison, Tom Kuchel, Gabriela Nosari, Kent Peterson, and Alice Tetelman for their wonderful support and goodwill. Carol Clark, the copy editor for this book, was a delight to work with, and Corrine Bartholomew did a great job in assisting with the manuscript.

I also want to thank all those associated with the State Policy Academy on Rural Competitiveness, especially the team leaders: Rod Armstrong, Nebraska; William Dickinson, Jr. and Neal Barber, Virginia; Rick Egged and Daniel

Orodenker, Hawaii; William Garcia and Elizabeth Martin, New Mexico; Richard Gardner, Idaho; and Paul Miner, California; and the coach/facilitators for these teams: Steve Adams, Joe Barker, Cynthia Clancy, Tom Henderson, Tom Unruh and Beverly Wilson. I have learned much from each of them.

Support for the CGPA State Policy Academy on Rural Competitiveness and for this book came from the Ford Foundation, the Aspen Institute, and the W.K. Kellogg Foundation. I want to express my gratitude as well to the people at each of these organizations for providing such warm support and encouragement during my work in this field: Dr. E. Walter Coward, Jr. and Chris Page at the Ford Foundation; T. Meriwether Jones, Maureen Kennedy, and Nancy Stark at the Aspen Institute; and Dr. Thomas L. Thorburn at the Kellogg Foundation. The contributions of the lead governors on this project, Terry E. Branstad of Iowa and Michael Sullivan of Wyoming, are appreciated.

My deepest appreciation goes to Dewitt John, who pointed me in a most promising direction; to Mark Popovich, who worked much longer than I to blaze the trail and clear the brush from this promising path; and to Alice Tetelman, who gave me the opportunity to take this journey.

As an avid reader, I had long wondered whether those acknowledged by the authors had actually made valuable contributions. There should be no doubt here. My sincere appreciation goes to the others, in addition to most of those mentioned above, who read the draft manuscript, offered thoughtful suggestions, and valiantly tried to prevent my making mistakes: Steve Buttress, Joseph Cortright, Raymond Cox, Richard Gross, Karen Kahn, Don Macke, Julie Marx, William Nothdurft, Edwin Parker, John Redman, and Richard Silkman. Notwithstanding the assistance of so many, the author alone is responsible for any error of fact or interpretation contained in this book.

Thanks also to Stephen Kahn Bonnett for so graciously yielding his time on "paintbrush" so that I could use the family computer.

PREFACE

Vast stretches of rural America constitute what might be called the orphan stepchildren of our modern body politic. Statistically, rural America, like Cinderella, is much poorer than her wealthier sisters — the cities and the suburbs. Rural communities are often neglected in national policy debates; rural America seldom receives national attention for either its major accomplishments or its chronic problems. Even its basic character is misunderstood because the general public still equates rural areas with agriculture. Much of rural America has pressing needs and lacks the fiscal capacity to address them adequately. It has no collective voice; its elected officials are divided among various ideologies.

The people struggling in rural communities represent far more than a contemporary version of our romantic nostalgia about virtuous life in the country. They also represent the pressing challenge that many of us face as we search for ways to adapt to rapidly changing economic and social forces without sacrificing our valued traditions of family, mutual support, and community.

Historically, rural economies in this country have been based upon natural resources industries — agriculture, forestry, mining, and fishing — and, in recent decades, upon low-wage manufacturing firms, especially in the South. Owing to the increasing global competition during the past decade, these sectors have been substituting capital inputs for labor to improve productivity. Employment in these sectors, consequently, has declined, and the prospect for future growth is not promising.

Although some rural economies have enjoyed strong growth from tourism, recreation, and urban expansion during the past decade, a much larger number have not. The much heralded rural renaissance of the 1970s was not sustained throughout the 1980s. During the 1980s, rural America lost population, its employment growth was much slower than that of urban areas, and the ratio of rural to urban wage levels declined, even for those at the same level of educational attainment.

State policymakers concerned about the future viability of their rural economies are now facing difficult choices about appropriate economic development strategies. In addition, the community leaders in many rural areas are becoming demoralized about their discouraging prospects for economic viability.

State governments, despite severe fiscal stress, represent the greatest promise for addressing the chronic problems of rural communities for three reasons: state governments bear dual responsibilities to preserve communities and provide essential services to improve the quality of peoples' lives; during the past two decades, the federal government has expanded its people-oriented responsibilities but has diluted its place-oriented programs; and far too many rural communities lack the institutional and financial capacity to make their own strategic investments to improve their economic viability. In short, they need special assistance from state governments.

The premise of this book is that we should care about the future of rural communities and that public policy should reflect this social concern. It describes the economic challenges facing rural economies because of global competition and national economic restructuring, addresses the rationale for public interventions to enhance the vitality of rural economies, summarizes trends in state economic development policies, and suggests several broad strategies that state policymakers may wish to consider that hold some promise of providing a healthy and prosperous future for rural communities. It also describes the process used by fifteen states that participated in the 1990 and 1992 CGPA State Policy Academies in developing public policies to advance rural competitiveness strategies.

The focus of this book is on the strategies of state governments, working in concert with community leadership, to improve rural competitiveness. Achieving vibrant, competitive rural economies is an important policy objective for state policymakers, but it cannot be met without extraordinary community leadership. Success in this mission would strengthen these collaborative relationships and provide resources that are essential in responding to other social needs and in achieving other community objectives.

The Competitive Challenqe for Rural Economies

M ore than ever, future rural economic progress depends on shrinking the "space" between urban and rural places and people, which will test the adequacy of the rural physical and institutional infrastructure. It may also require a substantial shift in the horizons of rural business people and public officials who need to see their future development in terms of broad forces of change in the marketplace. Distance and tradition cannot be relied upon to insulate local economies from structural change.

The challenge is to find ways of linking remote rural areas more fully into the national and global marketplace so that they can reduce their continuing dependence on economic sectors that are stagnant or declining in employment.   — Kenneth L. Deavers[1]

As Kenneth Deavers of the USDA's Economic Research Service observed, many rural communities face a serious economic challenge. Increasing global competition and the restructuring of America's economy threaten their future economic viability. To clarify this economic challenge, this chapter summarizes recent national and international economic trends, and a short review of how rural economies have evolved to their current stages of development. The second chapter discusses various rationales for public intervention to assist rural economies, and the third chapter summarizes general trends in state economic development policies. Strategic responses to the economic challenge are addressed in chapter 4.

Global competitiveness means that a greater percentage of what is produced and consumed locally or nationally has become competitive with other goods and services throughout the world. It means that with the exception of a small bundle of personal and household services, virtually everything we consume could be produced, and is being produced, in many parts of the globe. The label "Made in U.S.A.," sadly, no longer implicitly symbolizes a superior product; firms throughout the world have been successful in producing and marketing high-quality products that are competitive with those produced domestically. In addition, many U.S. firms have shifted some of their production facilities to other countries in recent years.

Many domestic goods and services do not have inherent cost advantages. One fact makes this telling point: in 1960 approximately 20 percent of our gross national product was subjected to competition from abroad, but now more than 70 percent of the nation's goods and services are subject to international competition.[2] Barring an international trade war, this percentage is not likely to decline in the future.

Many businesses and communities are experiencing the shock of emerging from a protective environment that had been sheltered, secure, and passive. Competitors have emerged from all corners of the globe. Capital and, to a lesser extent, technology have become so mobile that some businesses can flourish from virtually any site. Robert Reich, formerly a teacher at Harvard University's Kennedy School of Government and now secretary of labor in the Clinton administration, has noted that:

> Money, technology, information, and goods are flowing across national boundaries with unprecedented rapidity and ease. The cost of transporting things and communicating ideas is plummeting. Capital controls in most industrialized countries are being removed; trade barriers, reduced.[3]

The trends of increasingly mobile capital and accelerated international competition have caused tremendous changes in our society. As consumers, we each benefit from the improved products and lower prices that result from increased global competition. As concerned citizens, however, we are disturbed that domestic companies may lack the ability to innovate and compete successfully in the global market. Indeed, Laura D'Andrea Tyson wrote, before she was chosen to be the chairwoman of the president's Council of Economic Advisors, that "Our economic competitiveness — defined as our ability to produce goods and services that meet the test of international markets while our citizens enjoy a standard of living that is both rising and sustainable — is in slow but perceptible decline."[4]

America is one of the wealthiest nations in the world, but its living standards have not continued to improve as rapidly since 1973 as they had between the end of World War II and 1973. American productivity, defined as output per unit of input, is the highest in the world, but its growth in recent decades has been at a lower rate than that of many of our strongest competitors. Slow productivity growth is a major cause for concern: our future living standards will be determined by our level of productivity — the ability to produce goods and services with increasing efficiency.[5] In addition, the distribution of income and wealth has grown less equal during the 1980s.[6] These are among the primary concerns of the public as the national economy becomes restructured to compete in global markets. (Box 1-1 presents a summary of the forces underlying the global economy.)

Many economists and business analysts have argued that the national

Box 1-1
Forces Underlying the Global Economy

- The growing similarity of countries, with respect to tastes as well as to infrastructure, distribution channels, and marketing approaches.

- The emergence of a global capital market as witnessed by large flows of funds between countries.

- Declining tariff barriers and the establishment of regional trading agreements.

- Shifting opportunities for competitive advantage due to technology restructuring.

- The integrating role of advanced information and communication technologies.

- Slow and uneven world economic growth that has fanned the flames of international competitiveness.

- The emergence of new global competitors, principally from East Asia.

Source: Michael E. Porter, ed., *Competition in Global Industries* (Boston: Harvard Business School Press, 1986), 405 as quoted in *Rural America at the Crossroads: Networking for the Future*, U.S. Congress, Office of Technology Assessment, OTA-TCT-471 (Washington, D.C.: U.S. Government Printing Office, 1991), 50.

economy will continue to be globally competitive in high value-added manufacturing industries, advanced technologies, and specialized service industries such as entertainment.[7] They may be correct, but there has been scant evidence lately to justify overconfidence. The loss of market shares in automobiles, steel, airplanes, electronics, and other household items to companies in Japan, Germany, and other nations during the 1970s and 1980s has posed a serious economic challenge to our domestic firms and their employees.[8] (Box 1-2 presents an interpretation of how our domestic economy is being restructured in response to these globally competitive pressures.)

Box 1-2
What Is the New Economy?

In the old economy, nations competed principally on the basis of productivity and prices. Our success as a nation was measured by our ability to produce higher volumes of goods and services with the same or fewer resources. In the new economy, our national competitiveness is based not only on productivity, but also on quality, variety, customization, convenience, and timeliness. People are demanding high-quality goods and services that are competitively priced, available in a variety of forms, customized to specific needs, and conveniently accessible. What's more, people don't want to wait patiently for state-of-the-art products and services...in the global economy, if American industry doesn't meet these standards, somebody else will.... As new economic and technical forces change the standards for economic competition, they also affect organizational structures, skill requirements, and jobs. Organizational formats are shifting toward flexible networks that use information to integrate organizations, expedite strategic changes, and improve customer service. In fact, the physical energy necessary to extract resources, manufacture products, and deliver services is becoming less important than the information required to respond to markets quickly. *Increasingly, information is becoming the basic raw material of economic processes and the end product of economic activity.* (Emphasis added.)

Source: America and the New Economy by Anthony Patrick Carnevale (Alexandria, Va.: The American Society for Training and Development/ U.S. Department of Labor, 1991), 1-2.

The fate of routine manufacturing, which requires low skill levels, is much less promising in this country because of the increased global competition and lower wage levels of the rapidly industrializing nations. Firms in countries with cheaper labor than in the United States are successfully competing in apparel, textiles, printing, and other routine production industries. Multinational firms, regardless of where their headquarters may be located, are increasingly shifting these production operations to lower-wage countries. This is a particularly ominous trend for those rural economies dependent upon routine production industries to provide substantial employment.[9]

A growing sector of the national economy — producer services — has also become competitive globally. The advanced technologies that enabled Citibank to locate some of its credit card operations in South Dakota has enabled other domestic companies to locate keypunching and other service operations in India and Ireland.[10] Indeed, virtually any English-speaking community in the world with available workers who have basic language and math skills could provide certain back-office functions for large U.S. companies. According to a December 1992 *Fortune* article, typing mills in the Philippines can enter text and numbers into a computer for fifty cents per ten thousand characters — approximately five pages, double spaced — and a consultant has found a firm in China that charges only twenty cents for this service.[11]

No longer can one assume that back-office functions will be located domestically, nor that the lower-cost, higher quality-of-life aspects of rural communities will succeed in attracting this employment. As will be discussed later, rural communities must obtain state-of-the-art telecommunication systems and prepare their workers for new tasks and responsibilities to be successful in the competition for employment opportunities.

The recent literature on globalization suggests that functions beyond routine manufacturing and service operations are also dispersing throughout the world. Cost advantages account for some of this fundamental shift; also significant are the rising educational levels in many rapidly industrializing nations as well as the desire to locate business operations "in markets that promise the most growth." The *Fortune* article catalogued evidence of this phenomenon: 3M making pressure-sensitive tapes, chemicals, and electrical parts in Bangalore, India, and *Texas Instruments, Motorola*, and *IBM* establishing software programming nearby; *Hewlett-Packard* assembling computers and designing memory boards in Guadalajara, Mexico; *Quarterdeck Office Systems* using multilingual workers to translate instruction manuals and software in Dublin, Ireland; *Metropolitan Life* employing educated workers in Fermoy, Ireland, to analyze medical insurance claims and review new policies sold by salesmen in the United States; and "In less than two years, more than 40 companies, including *AT&T, Thomson*, and *Sumitomo Electric Industries*, have established factories in the new (industrial) parks, chiefly on Batam Island," Indonesia. Hence, the author concluded that "A fundamental shift is under way in how and where the world's work gets done…. The key to this change: the emergence of a truly global labor force talented and capable of accomplishing just about anything, anywhere." [12]

How Does Global Competition Affect Rural Economies?

Most rural economies traditionally have been based on natural resource industries such as farming, forestry, fishing, or mining. During the last century, most rural economies changed significantly as natural resource industries became increasingly capital intensive, partly because of global competition, and their employment levels declined.

The history of increased agricultural productivity provides many examples of how better machines, new pesticides, and new techniques have led to declining employment. The settlement of the West during the nineteenth century threatened the prosperity of many small farms in the Northeast, which pushed many from the farms into the rapidly industrializing cities on the East Coast. Another prominent example was the introduction of the mechanical cotton picker in the South in 1944, which liberated tens of thousands from back-breaking manual labor but, in doing so, displaced them from their communities, leading to the search for jobs and opportunities in the northern cities.[13]

In 1893, when Grover Cleveland was president, 42 percent of the nation's population lived on farms; now, approximately 2 percent live on farms. Nationally, farming employment declined from 9.9 million in 1950 to less than three million today. Recent employment data for all nonmetropolitan counties reveals that farming now provides employment for fewer than one in ten rural workers.

Indeed, recent employment data demonstrate how much rural economies, in the aggregate, have shifted from these traditional resource-based industries and become more like the national economy: less than 12 percent of nonmetropolitan workers are now employed in agriculture, forestry, fishing, or mining. The contribution of these natural resource-based industries to the national economy has also declined steadily. In 1947, for example, agriculture, forestry, and fisheries represented approximately 9 percent of the gross national product, but this share fell to roughly 2 percent in 1989.[14] According to a 1990 U.S. Department of Labor report, only 3 percent of the U.S. population makes its living in farming, timbering, fishing, and mining.

Natural resource industries are the mainstay of many regional economies, but they are increasingly subject to stiff global competition. The value of these goods and the ability to export them are determined primarily by the value of the dollar and various trade policies and tariffs. Federal budgets and national trade policies have had and will continue to have significant impact on the development of these primary industries.

International strife, natural disasters, and catastrophes, and advanced technological and chemical improvements are each likely, in various and uncertain ways, to affect the future growth potential of each of these industries. Another oil embargo or energy crisis would help the domestic energy industry. An international trade war resulting in selective tariffs would, in the short term, boost the value of natural resources. A devalued American dollar would stimulate exported natural resources because they would be sold at cheaper prices (but it would reduce the purchasing power of consumers by making imports more expensive).

Nevertheless, it is difficult to imagine a set of circumstances in which employment in these natural resource-based industries could grow substantially in the future. The rural economies based on stable resource-based industries, roughly one-third of all rural counties, will require strategic investments to encourage diversity and growth in other sectors to strengthen their economies.

The gradual shift from natural resource-based industries led many rural communities to recruit manufacturing firms, which were searching for lower taxes and cheaper land and labor. This movement began in earnest in the 1950s and accelerated through the 1960s and 1970s. According to Deavers, "There are twice as many people in rural America employed in manufacturing as are employed in mining, energy, and farming combined." [15] Much of this employment is in routine manufacturing (requiring few skills), which faces severe competition from plants in foreign nations where labor and land costs are much cheaper. More than 30 percent of all rural manufacturing jobs during the mid-1980s were in apparel, textiles, wood products, leather, and shoes.[16]

An additional threat to some rural communities in the future is the loss of employment from businesses providing goods and services for mostly local markets that have thus far been isolated from outside competition. The introduction of Wal-Mart stores, for example, has jeopardized the existing retail sector in many small towns throughout the country.[17] Small firms in remote rural communities that are relatively isolated and disadvantaged by poor transportation systems could become subject to increased competition in the future. Local service providers such as accountants, lawyers, and tax advisers in rural communities may discover that the aggressive marketing by nonlocal firms, and the development of telecommunications systems, suddenly pose competitive threats.[18]

The combination of these factors led to growing disparities between rural and urban counties during the 1980s in these conditions:

- Higher increase in poverty in rural areas, resulting in a rural poverty rate nearly 50 percent higher than the urban poverty rate;

- A widening gap between median family income, as rural family income actually decreased in real terms;[19]

- Slower rural employment growth: nonmetro employment grew by 8 percent between 1979 and 1987 while metro employment grew 18 percent during this period;[20] and

- Rural counties lost population while urban counties grew during the decade; of particular concern, according to Kenneth Deavers, the rural outmigration was "not only age specific but education specific. As a consequence many of the rural citizens most important to future rural development are leaving rural America."[21]

If rural America experienced such difficulties during the 1980s — which included a period of steady national growth following the 1982 recovery — what are its future prospects? If global competition and the restructuring of the national economy are likely to limit the future expansion of employment in natural resource industries, jeopardize the future employment in routine manufacturing, and threaten existing rural businesses, what then are the opportunities for future economic viability for rural communities? Can't state and local governments do something to boost employment in natural resources industries? If routine manufacturing firms are facing such severe global competition, what are the implications for those rural communities that rely so heavily upon them for employment? What can the public sector do to help them compete? In short, what is to be done?

These questions will be addressed later in the book, but first the concept of "rural" merits additional attention. Government agencies and scholars generally define urban places and then define all nonmetropolitan areas as rural areas (see box 1-3). Most rural communities have low population density and are remote from metropolitan areas. Their economies pose special challenges owing to scale and weak links with the more vibrant urban, national, and international economies. These scarcely populated, remote rural communities constitute the majority of rural places, but are home to a small percentage of all rural Americans. For example, approximately three-fourths of all rural residents live in counties that are either adjacent to a metropolitan area — within fifty miles of a metro core population—or have urbanized populations of twenty thousand or more. This latter set of rural communities, in general, confronts fewer obstacles to developing diversified economies.

The economic problems of the more remote parts of rural America pose a special challenge. Mark Drabenstott, the vice president of the Kansas City Federal Reserve Bank, has observed that "many parts of rural America are disconnected…. Can we in some way put rural areas in touch with the metropolitan areas that are centers of innovation, or technology, of finance, and of social and cultural amenities?" [22] This distinction — between the more remote rural areas and those surrounding urban centers — is key to the following discussion about the challenges facing rural economies.

Challenges for Rural Economies

Responding to the challenge of global competition will require strategies based upon the comparative advantages of different regions, linkages with nearby metropolitan areas, and core economic strengths. As discussed in chapter 5, the process of conducting a strategic assessment of these key conditions is an important first step toward designing strategic policy responses. The following is, by necessity, an overview of some of the conceptual challenges facing most rural economies.

Opportunities sometime result from chance — more often, they result from devising an effective strategy to exploit one's strength or comparative advantages in a competitive context. Opportunities also result from well-designed strategies to overcome disadvantages, barriers, or obstacles that thwart optimal performance or limit viable options.

Several economists who have studied rural economies have identified three major disadvantages that limit economic growth. The first of these is the *distance penalty*. Goods produced in rural areas have a price disadvantage because they must be transported, at considerable expense, to far away markets.[23] During most of our nation's history, improving the flow of goods to market was the leading rural development strategy. This was especially true during the nineteenth century, beginning with the Erie Canal in New York, continuing with Henry Clay's leadership for roads and internal improvements in the West, and, later, the aggressive expansion of railroads throughout the country, which is discussed in chapter 2.

Canals, railroads, and good roads have been extremely important in minimizing the distance penalty. Indeed, the development of the national interstate highway system was one of the key factors that enabled so much

Box 1-3
What Is Rural?

The remarkable diversity of rural areas in this country has posed a challenge to the ability of researchers to devise meaningful classification systems. One classification system developed by the Economic Research Service placed all nonmetropolitan counties into three broad categories: urbanized (those having an urban population of at least twenty thousand) less urbanized (those having an urban population of 2,555 to 19,999) and rural (those with no places of 2,500 or more population). Within each of these three categories, it grouped nonmetropolitan counties by those *adjacent* to a metropolitan county and those *nonadjacent* to a metropolitan county.

Another classification system, developed by the researchers at the Economic Research Service in 1985, placed nonmetropolitan counties into seven social and economic categories: farming, manufacturing, mining, specialized government, persistent poverty, federal lands, and destination-retirement.

To the lament of rural advocates, two federal agencies define rural areas as those remaining after metropolitan areas are defined. The Office of Management and Budget (OMB) first defines metropolitan counties (MSAs); those remaining are nonmetropolitan counties, which are those lacking a city of at least fifty thousand or a commuting connection with a city of that size. Of the 3,097 counties in the United States, 2,388 — or 77 percent — are nonmetropolitan. The Census Bureau has a more comprehensive definition of urban which includes: cities of 50,000 or more along with adjacent jurisdictions having a density of 1000 persons per square mile and other urban places (those with 2000 or more residents). According to this definition, rural areas are all other nonurban areas. Other federal agencies, naturally, have different definitions of rural areas. For example, according to a textbook, *Rural Communities: Legacy and Change* (p.7):

> The Farmers Home Administration (FmHA) defines rural areas as open country, communities of up to 20,000 residents in nonmetropolitan areas, and towns of up to 10,000 having a rural character but located within metropolitan counties. Agencies that deal with transportation issues define rural communities as those with populations of fewer than 5,000.

The standard use of data from nonmetropolitan counties to describe and analyze the problems of rural America — which is done here as well — poses an unavoidable problem. Many counties within standard metropolitan areas (MSAs) have small towns and rural areas, but the data on those populations are included with the metropolitan counties. Excluding the rural areas within metropolitan counties from the description of rural America produces a distorted portrait. In 1980, for example, 40 percent of the rural population lived in MSAs, which meant those data were included in the metropolitan county data; also, 14 percent of the MSA population lived in rural areas, as defined by the Census Bureau.

In addition to multiple definitions, the number in various categories changes after every census. For example, the metropolitan spread during most of this century has transformed formerly rural counties into urban ones, reducing the number of rural counties after each decennial census.

Having so many definitions is quite confusing; in addition, many state governments may also define or classify rural areas differently. *It may be helpful for state policymakers and rural advocates to discuss what they mean by rural; developing a consensus definition may guide further discussion and subsequent policy development.*

Source: Cornelia Butler Flora, Jan L. Flora, Jacqueline D. Spears, Louis E. Swanson with Mark B. Lapping and Mark L. Weinberg, *Rural Communities: Legacy and Change*, (Boulder, Colo.: Westview Press, 1992), 7-13; See also David A. McGranahan, J.C. Hession, F.K. Hines, and M.F. Jordon, *Social and Economic Characteristics of the Population in Metro and Nonmetropolitan Counties*, 1970-1980, Rural Development Research Report No.58, (Washington, D.C.: U.S. Department of Agriculture, Economic Research Service, 1986); and L.D. Bender, B.L. Green, T.F. Hady, J.A. Kuehn, M.K. Nelson, L.B. Perkinson, and P.J. Ross, *The Diverse Social and Economic Structure of Nonmetropolitan America*, Rural Development Research Report No. 49, (Washington, D.C.: U.S. Department of Agriculture, Economic Research Service, 1985).

routine manufacturing to relocate to rural areas during the 1960s and 1970s. Yet, the national economic restructuring from primarily hard goods production toward producing "soft" goods and services should lead one to think differently about the concept of a rural distance penalty.

Minimizing the distance penalty in our information-dominated economy does not mean simply building better roads: it means having reasonable access both to airports and to the prominent metropolitan areas of the region; single party touchtone calling and line quality that can reliably transmit voice, data, and facsimile messages; and informal social networks that provide opportunities for professionals and managers to exchange information, ideas, and concepts and to explore potential innovations.[24]

Advanced technologies and progressive telecommunication policies could, theoretically, overcome much of the traditional disadvantage of a distance penalty for rural communities. The distance penalty used to refer to the physical distance to and from the markets; now the distance penalty measures the ability to exchange information about products, services, and technologies with nearby urban economies and global markets. Minimizing the social, cultural, and psychological isolation of these communities is an equally significant task, however.

The second disadvantage of rural economies is their relative *lack of scale economies* because of low population density. The concept of economies of scale explains the increased productivity from mass production operations. A related concept — positive externalities — occurs when firms benefit from locating within a cluster of similar firms and suppliers. From the perspective of a rural community, the concept of scale economies means having sufficient access to labor, capital, other resources, supplies, suppliers, and technologies to operate a business or businesses efficiently.[25]

Firms that need many specially skilled workers, particularly obscure materials, or unique services may not choose to locate in most rural communities. Some rural communities are so remote and scarcely populated that they are not realistic sites for specific economic activities. Nevertheless, the historic rural disadvantage of economies of scale, stemming from low population densities, may be diminished in the future by advances in telecommunications technology and the nature of national economic restructuring. Consider these two reasons:

- Manufacturing today provides just 17 percent of the nation's employment, down from 35 percent in 1950. The traditional concept of scale economies may be less valid in many industries because the nature of manufacturing is changing. Recent trends suggest that modern forms of manufacturing, owing to technology and decentralization, are evolving away from the mass production model for many high value-added goods. These new forms are called flexible, lean, or agile production and require advanced technology and highly skilled workers.[26]

- The growing service sector — which includes retail and wholesale trade, hotel and tourist operations, financial, health, legal, and government services — provides more than 60 percent of the national employment. It is unclear whether low population densities represents a significant disadvantage for the development of many enterprises in the growing service sector. The proliferation of personal computers, facsimile machines, satellite systems, computer bulletin boards, and other systems have increasingly enabled various service sector firms to compete vigorously in any location, including rural ones.

In the past, a firm that required many highly specialized support services might have been reluctant to locate in a small town, but modern telecommunication technologies have made this a reasonable option. A publishing company might have believed, for example, that it needed frequent direct contact with copyright attorneys, but now these services can be provided through modem, facsimile, or videoconference. An essay by Don A. Dillman provides these examples of how information technologies have been used in rural settings to overcome the distance penalty — effectively nullifying the concept of scale economies:

> A telemarketing firm in Breda, Iowa, a computer software firm in Ketchum, Idaho, an employment search firm in Missoula, Montana, a national cookie firm in Park City, Utah, an upscale candy manufacturer in Durango, Colorado, accounting firms in rural Mississippi, and various telemarketers in South Central Nebraska. National clothing marketers in central Maine and southern Wisconsin are other examples. Some of these businesses were homegrown; others were brought to their locations by entrepreneurs seeking an escape from their metropolitan locations in search of a preferred lifestyle.[27]

A *Forbes* article entitled "The Virtual Workplace" observed that "The explosive advances in telecommunications and computing make the hinterlands ever closer." The article quoted a real estate consultant who concluded that "Geography is irrelevant" and gave examples of companies that moved offices or certain back office functions "to accommodate the preferences of either their current employees or the kinds of employees they would like to hire in the future." It also described a commercial system — of tremendous potential to rural economies —

That automatically routes incoming calls to a customer service line to multiple locations, allowing companies to staff their 800 numbers with operators in different places to time zones. For instance, if you call an appliance service center in Sacramento, California, to ask when your washer/dryer will be delivered, a part-time worker in Salt Lake City, working the swing shift from her living room while the kids are in school, may pick up the phone. And she can pull up your record on her terminal and tell you the time it was placed on the truck 200 miles away and when the estimated time of delivery will be.[28]

(For more on this topic, see box 1-4.)

Box 1-4
Scale Economies for Diversified Rural Economies?

Some rural development scholars think that the low population densities of rural communities will restrict their ability to diversify their economies and prevent them from developing producer services. Kenneth Deavers has articulated this concern:

> Rural areas didn't do at all well in the 1980s in producer services, which was an enormously productive growth sector for the U.S. economy. Those are services that earn exports for local economies because they are sold to markets that are regional, national, or global. Without export earnings, the service sector can't be an engine for future growth, any more than the goods-production sector could have been in the past.
>
> Economists have grossly underestimated the importance in the producer service sector of agglomeration economies and of face-to-face ways of doing business. We have been enamored of new technologies that allow people to do business from a distance. We have failed to understand that those technologies only work if you also, very often and reasonably cheaply, can meet directly with your clients.[29]

The third disadvantage of rural economies is their *poor infrastructure*. Rural communities, in general, have less wealth than urban or suburban communities. The local tax base of most rural communities is weak, disproportionately finances local schools, and often is heavily burdened by federal standards for water, sewage, and waste disposal systems. Many do not have the fiscal capacity either to make important infrastructure improvements in their communities to improve the quality of life (to the level enjoyed by most suburban residents, for example) or to enhance the economic attractiveness of their communities. The chronic fiscal weakness of rural communities — constraining their ability to make essential infrastructure investments, repairs, and improvements — is likely to remain one of the more significant economic disadvantages to rural competitiveness in the foreseeable future.

Agglomeration economies is the term that explains the advantages that firms have from locating in close proximity to many others. The positive external benefits resulting from both firms and workers from different industries locating in close proximity and the "synergy" from these interactions is a common explanation for cities. Urban economic textbooks list access to a common labor market, various business services and suppliers, information business networks, and professional face-to-face interactions as advantages of agglomeration economics.[30] (Industry clusters also occur in rural areas: the furniture industry in Tuperlin, Mississippi, carpet manufacturers in Dalton, Georgia, and metalworking firms near Gadsten, Alabama.)[31]

Our domestic cities clearly had technological and agglomeration advantages in developing producer services during the 1980s. Will those advantages continue? How important are the positive externalities of urban environments to the growing sectors of the national economy? At what point do the negative externalities of urban environments — such as crime, disorder, high taxes, congestion, inferior air quality, poor education and public services — outweigh the positive economic advantages? How important are *frequent* meetings "directly with clients?" Will this obstacle also be minimized by future technologies? [32]

Rural Advantages for Future Competitiveness

One of the strongest advantages of rural communities is their environments. With some exceptions, rural communities have much cleaner air and water than most urban or suburban communities. By definition, the lack of population density provides surroundings of physical space, less congestion, and often remarkable natural beauty. It is difficult to describe, and impossible to quantify, the strong bond many rural Americans feel toward the land. The growth of tourism throughout rural America serves as testimony that most urban Americans seek and value this elemental connection with nature as well.

Rural communities often have unique amenities that provide economic advantages such as lakes, rivers, mountains, seashores, natural beauty, and scenic wonders, special vegetation or wildlife, historic landmarks and artifacts, or representations of diverse cultures. William A. Galston, coauthor of a forthcoming book on the future of rural development, has observed that "The kinds of natural characteristics regarded as "amenity values" by retirees, vacationers, and certain businesses have emerged as the chief new source of rural comparative advantage." [33] These unique resources are clearly very important economic assets and should be developed in prudent, sustainable fashion. As valuable as they are now, they are likely to become far more valuable, if current trends continue, in the future.

Related to this concept of superior environment are other rural attributes: the slower pace of life, greater mutual support from friends and neighbors, more voluntary civic activities, less crime and disorder, and a greater sense of community pride. Indeed, some rural communities may have a distinct advantage in the future because of these attributes. In fact, a 1992 Roper public opinion survey revealed that more Americans preferred to live in a small town or rural area — although most do not — than any other setting. [34]

According to this survey, most Americans view "rural America as the place to find a better quality of life, defined by elements such as cost of living, personal values, traffic congestion, freedom from pollution, overall quality of life, and better condition of streets and roads." Significantly, the survey also indicated three reasons that more people were not choosing a rural way of life:

- Most people are satisfied with the amenities and quality of life in their own communities;

- Rural America is perceived as lacking services (such as health care, police protection, quality education, entertainment) and cultural opportunities that many value; and

- Rural America is thought to provide much fewer career opportunities than other settings: "Rural Americans are thought to have the least opportunity of any group asked about to achieve the "American Dream" — fewer opportunities than even low-income Americans or recent immigrants — while big city dwellers are thought to have more opportunities than most Americans." [35]

Sociologists have used the term, *Gemeinschaft*, to define the concept of community often associated with life in small towns and sparsely populated areas:

> Members of a community are relatively immobile in a physical and social way: individuals neither travel far from their locality of birth nor do they rise up the social hierarchy. In addition, the culture of the community is relatively homogeneous, for it must be so if roles are not to conflict or human relations to lose their intimacy. The moral custodians of a community, the family and the church, are strong, their code clear and their injunctions well internalized. There will be community sentiments involving close and enduring loyalties to the place and people....[36]

Many in our modern society will find these community attributes too restrictive and confining. Others, however, will value them. The movement of retirees to rural communities during the last two decades suggests that these community attributes have been valued by this cohort. Will they appeal to other demographic groups in the future? Should these community attributes of rural areas be marketed to selective groups? If rural communities were able to provide quality public services and had diverse job opportunities, would they be more attractive to current residents of metropolitan areas? Attractive enough to motivate relocation?

An important economic advantage for rural economies is the general consensus that the work ethic is strong and dependable and the work force is independent and proud of its productivity. It is difficult to quantify these attributes of rural workers compared with urban ones. Nevertheless, the popular perception of a hardworking labor force is a very important economic advantage for rural communities that should be emphasized.

It is conventional wisdom that the lower cost of land in most rural areas compared with most metropolitan areas is another important comparative advantage for most rural economies. This will continue to be a distinct advantage for some firms and merits emphasis by the promoters of rural communities. Yet, in some respects, the domestic comparative advantages that rural communities have — in terms of lower land and labor costs than those of metropolitan areas — are becoming less relevant.[37]

Most rural communities are not fundamentally in competition with urban America nor are they competing among themselves to foster greater business and employment opportunities as the national economy is restructured. Rural communities are increasingly *competing for jobs and incomes with all other locations throughout the world*; land costs in rural America are hardly cheaper than land in the least developed nations of the world, which also have much cheaper labor costs. In a striking parallel, the telecommunications systems and technological advances that have done so much to diminish the distance penalty for rural America may have also partly eliminated its historic advantage of low land costs because now an increasing range of economic functions — from mass production to back-office tasks — can be done in many places throughout the world. Why would mass production facilities or back-office functions be enticed by cheap land in rural communities when they increasingly are choosing sites for relocation or expansion in the lower wage, rapidly industrializing nations?

This topic serves as another opportunity to reframe the challenge facing rural communities in the context of global competition and national economic structuring. To use a historical example, the efficiency of James Watt's steam engine in the nineteenth century liberated industrial activities from locations providing water power.[38] Today telecommunications and other advanced technologies are the historical equivalent of Watt's steam engine: they enable the dispersal of most information-based economic functions regardless of geography — just as the steam engine enabled industrial activity to locate away from water power. This simultaneously minimizes the historic disadvantage of the distance penalty, which potentially could increase economic activity in rural America, and, paradoxically, places these communities in direct competition with the rest of world.

Similarly, the mass production techniques advanced by Henry Ford earlier in this century required modestly skilled labor and large tracts of land, which gradually led many of these operations — aided by the Interstate Highway system — to relocate from urban areas to where both land and labor was much cheaper. Yet today a much smaller percentage of our national wealth is created through mass production and much of this is speeding rapidly to the lower wage, industrializing nations. *Cheap land and cheaper labor costs, in domestic terms, were yesterday's comparative advantages for rural communities; tomorrow's comparative advantages, in a globally competitive environment, could be the work ethic and skill levels of rural workers; the quality of rural America's telecommunications infrastructure; and the adaptability and flexibility of rural communities to changing economic conditions.*

The next chapter will discuss various rationales for public intervention to improve rural competitiveness, chapter 3 will summarize trends in state economic development policies, and chapter 4 will describe various strategies by state governments to improve the competitiveness of rural economies. Developing appropriate state policies, though, begins with understanding the immediate economic challenge threatening rural communities: the sectors that have provided historically the most employment — natural resources industries and routine manufacturing — are experiencing global competition. The longer-term trend is for these sectors to become more productive as capital is invested (and as technology is developed), but that will further reduce employment.

The nation's governors and other state government leaders who are concerned about the economic viability of their rural communities must think strategically about how to assist them to become more competitive. Working closely with the leadership of rural communities, they should begin by communicating directly with rural residents to explain this immediate economic challenge. Kenneth Deavers has used the word "remoteness" to describe how difficult this task may be:

> Rural people don't understand very well what is happening in the global and national economy that is playing out to their disadvantage in their communities. These rural people are disconnected institutionally. They are disconnected in a number of other ways, and they just don't have easy access. They are remote from understanding the things that are affecting their future, and that is important.[39]

Notes:

1. Kenneth L. Deavers, "1980's A Decade of Broad Rural Stress," *Rural Development Perspectives* 7, no. 3 (June-September 1991): 5.

2. Robert Friedman, "Rural Economic Development in the 1990s: The Changing State Role" (Paper prepared for presentation at the CGPA State Policy Academy on Rural Competitiveness, May 1992), 17.

See also Doug Ross and Robert E. Friedman, "The Emerging Third Wave: New Economic Development Strategies" in R. Scott Fosler, ed., *Local Economic Development: Strategies for a Changing Economy*, (Washington, D.C,: International City Management Association, 1991), 126.

3. Robert B. Reich, *The Work of Nations* (New York: Vintage Books/Random House, 1992), 6-7. In addition to Reich's many examples of this phenomenon, Richard Rothstein in *Keeping Jobs in Fashion: Alternatives to the Euthanasia of the U.S. Apparel Industry* (Washington, D.C.:

Economic Policy Institute, 1989), 48, wrote that the number of garment production facilities in Bangladesh jumped from 40 in 1984 to 545 in 1985 because Hong Kong had reached its quota limits and sought offshore operations to produce for the U.S. market.

4. Laura D'Andrea Tyson, *Who's Bashing Whom?: Trade Conflict in High-Technology Industries* (Washington, D.C.: Institute for International Economics, 1993), 1. For more on this theme, see Lester C. Thurow, *Head to Head: The Coming Economic Battle Among Japan, Europe, and America* (New York: Morrow, 1992); Robert B. Reich, The Work of Nations; and Paul Krugman, *The Age of Diminished Expectations: U.S. Economic Policy in the 1990s*, (Cambridge, Mass.: MIT Press, 1992).

5. See *American Living Standards: Threats and Challenges*, ed., Robert E. Litan, Robert Z. Lawrence, and Charles L. Schultze (Washington, D.C.: Brookings, 1988); Edward F. Denison, *Trends in American Economic Growth*, 1919-1982 (Washington, D.C.: Brookings, 1985) in which Denison emphasizes the important distinction between the conventional measure of labor productivity (output per worker) and total factor productivity (output per factor input), see pp.22-30; and Robert Z. Lawrence, *Can America Compete?* (Washington, D.C.: The Brookings Institution, 1984).

6. See Paul R. Krugman, "The Rich, the Right, and the Facts," *The American Prospect* no.11 (Fall 1992): 19-31 for a liberal view of this controversy.

7. See Reich (1992), Lawrence (1984), Krugman, *Age of Diminished Expectations*, 1992, Thurow (1992), and Michael Porter, *The Competitive Advantage of Nations* (New York: Basic Books, 1990).

8. Reich (1992) has argued forcefully that most firms competitive in global markets necessarily have less national allegiance than they had formerly when most of their goods and services were sold in domestic markets. Hence, from a policy perspective, it matters much less now than previously: who owns which firms, where their headquarters are, and how and where they make investments decisions to remain competitive. Consider this section from page 3 of his introduction:

> We are living through a transformation that will rearrange the politics and economics of the coming century. There will be no *national* products or technologies, no national corporations, no national industries. There will no longer be national economies, at least as we have come to understand that concept. All that will remain rooted within national borders are the people who comprise a nation. Each nation's primary assets will be its citizens' skills and insights. (Original emphasis.)

Reich may be correct in this vision of the future; long-term trends support this view. Currently, however, nations still have borders, and within nations are different cultures that have influenced corporate management decisions. Reich earlier had raised questions about the emerging phenomenon of the Japanese-American corporation in *Tales of a New America: The Anxious Liberal's Guide to the Future* (New York: Vintage Books, 1988), 80:

> The emerging Japanese-American corporation is problematic in this regard, for although it invests diligently in the skills of Japanese workers, it tends to shortchange American workers. As we shall observe, this is not because of any nefarious motive on the part of the Japanese; it is rather a function of the different ethical and economic premises they bring to corporate activity.

Responding to this and other concerns, Krugman, *Age of Diminished Expectations*, 1992, concluded that (pp.126-127):

Japanese firms already here pay wages as high or higher than both American firms and other foreign firms in the United States; they also do just as much R&D. Unfortunately, the third charge is true: Japanese firms do seem to import a lot more, most of it presumably from Japanese suppliers, than either U.S. firms or other foreign firms.

For more on this topic, see Laura D'Andrea Tyson, "They Are Not Us: Why American Ownership Still Matters," and Robert B. Reich, "Rejoinder: Who Do We Think They Are," *The American Prospect* no.4 (Winter 1991): 37-53. See also Laura D'Andrea Tyson, *Who's Bashing Whom?: Trade Conflict in High-Technology Industries*, (Washington, D.C.: Institute for International Economics, 1993).

9. See Krugman, *Age of Diminished Expectations*, 1992, Reich (1992), Thurow (1992) and Peter Dicken, *Global Shift: The Internationalization of Economic Activity*, (New York: The Guilford Press, 1992), 2d ed. Note also this concise summary by Aaron Berstein, Walecia Konrad and Lois Therrien, "The Global Economy: Who Gets Hurt," *Business Week*, 10 Aug. 1992, 51:

Wolfgang R. Stopler and Paul A. Samuelson, the father of neoclassical economics, first expressed the concept in 1941, with elegant equations that built on Ricardo's comparative advantage theory. If goods trade freely, the idea goes, prices will equalize, and so will production costs. To compete, countries must specialize where they have a relative edge. Low-wage countries will make labor-intensive goods, while those with capital will do better in technology-intensive products. Thus, U.S. low-skilled work should flow overseas, or wages of low-skilled workers must fall.

10. Reich (1992) and Brian O'Reilly "Your New Global Work Force," *Fortune* 126, no.13, (December 14, 1992).

11. O'Reilly, "Your New Global Work Force," 54.

12. Ibid.; For a good summary of some of the recent literature on globalization, see Michael Marien, *Future Survey* 14, no. 10 (October 1992). The average shopper may notice this phenomenon also. The last lightbulb the author purchased was made by General Electric in Korea, the sneakers were Reeboks made in Thailand, and the telephone was made by AT&T in Indonesia.

13. A particularly vivid account of the migration from the Mississippi delta to Chicago after World War II is presented in Nicholas Lemann, *The Promised Land*, (New York: Knopf, 1991).

14. Katherine Reichelderfer, "Natural Resources and Rural Development" (Presentation at the National Rural Economic Development Institute—a program for State Council Training supported by federal and state governments and the Cooperative Extension Service, University of Wisconsin under Special Project No. 90-EXCA-3-0116, March 3-7, 1991).

15. Kenneth L. Deavers, Presentation at GAO Symposium on Rural Development, June 1992; as quoted in *Rural Development: Rural America Faces Many Challenges* GAO/RCED-93-35, (Washington, D.C.: General Accounting Office, November 1992), 31; also see Deavers, "1980's A Decade of Broad Rural Stress" *Rural Development Perspectives*, no.3, (June-September 1991): 2-5.

16. David L. Brown and Kenneth L. Deavers, "The Changing Content of Rural Research and Policy," (unpublished paper) Economic Research Service, USDA, Washington, D.C., 1986, as quoted in Dewitt John, Sandra S. Batie, and Kim Norris, *A Brighter Future for Rural America: Strategies for Communities and States*, (Washington, D.C.: National Governors Association, 1988), 94.

17. For a thoughtful essay about how communities can respond to the invasion of a Wal-Mart, see Alan Ehrenhalt,"Up Against the Wal-Mart," *Governing* 5, no.12, (September 1992): 6-7. For a case study of how one small town may have become stronger after a Wal-Mart was built, see Donald Dale Jackson, "It's Wake-up Time for Main Street When Wal-Mart Comes to Town," *Smithsonian* 23, no.7 (October 1992): 36-47.

18. Edwin B. Parker and Heather E. Hudson, with Don A. Dillman, Sharon Strover, and Fredrick Williams, *Electronic Byways: State Policies for Rural Development through Telecommunications* (Boulder, Colo.:Westview Press/Aspen Institute, 1992), 27.

19. Cornelia B. Flora and James A. Christenson, "Critical Times for Rural America: The Challenge for Rural Policy in the 1990s," in *Rural Policies for the 1990s*, Cornelia B. Flora and James A. Christenson, eds. (Boulder, Colo.: Westview Press, 1992), 3.

20. S. Barancik, *The Rural Disadvantage: Growing Income Disparities between Rural and Urban Areas.* (Washington, D.C.:Center on Budget and Policy Priorities, 1990) as quoted in William A. Galston, "Rural America in the 1990s: Trends and Choices," *Policy Studies Journal 20*, no.2, (1992): 202.

21. Kenneth L. Deavers, "Rural development in the 1990s: Data and research needs" (Paper prepared for the Rural Social Science Symposium, American Agricultural Economics Association, Baton Rouge, Louisiana, July 1989); as quoted by William A. Galston, "Rural America in the 1990s, 203.

22. Mark Drabenstott, Presentation at the GAO Symposium on Rural Development, as quoted in *Rural Development: Rural America Faces Many Challenges* GAO/RCED-93-35, (Washington, D.C.: General Accounting Office, November 1992), 49.

23. Parker et al., *Electronic Byways*, 27-28.

24. Ibid., 3.

25. See Edwin S. Mills, *Urban Economics* (Glenview, Ill.: Scott, Foresman and Company, 1972), 13-14.

26. Doug Ross, "Enterprise Economics on the Front Lines: Empowering Firms and Workers to Win," In *Mandate for Change*, ed. Will Marshall and Martin Schram, (New York: Berkley/Progressive Policy Institute, 1993), 56.

27. Don A. Dillman, "Information Technologies and Rural Economic Development" in *National Rural Studies Committee: A Proceedings* (Corvallis, Oregon: Western Rural Development Center/ Oregon State University), Sponsored by W.K.Kellogg Foundation (May 14-16, 1992), 77. See also Allen Gilbert, "Access to the World: Telecommunications and Computers Offer Some New Opportunities," *Vermont Life* 46, no.3 (Spring 1992): 28-31. Note, however, of those profiled in the *Vermont Life* article, most had gained specialized expertise in urban environments before transferring their operations to Vermont settings. This phenomenon was also reported in Joseph Berger, "Rural Home, A City Job and a Modem," *New York Times*, 15 February 1993, B-1.

28. David C. Churbuck and Jeffery S. Young, "The Virtual Workplace," *Forbes* 150, no.12, (November 23, 1992): 184.

29. Kenneth L. Deavers, *Rural Development: Rural America Faces Many Challenges*, GAO/RCED-93-35 (Washington, D.C.: U.S. General Accounting Office, November 1992), 35-36.

30. See Jane Jacobs, *The Economy of Cities* (New York: Vintage Books/Random House, 1970); Jane Jacobs, *Cities and the Wealth of Nations*, (New York: Vintage Books/Random House, 1985); Edwin S. Mills, *Urban Economics*, (Glenview, Ill.: Scott, Foresman and Company, 1972); and Edwin S. Mills and John F. McDonald, eds. *Sources of Metropolitan Growth* (New Brunswick, N.J.: Center for Urban Policy Research, Rutgers, 1992).

31. John W. Harman, "Symposium's Results in Brief, in report entitled " *Rural Development: Rural America Faces Many Challenges* GAO/RCED-93-35, (Washington, D.C.: General Accounting Office, November 1992), 3.

32. The three most important things about real estate, according to the old joke, are location, location, and location. Jane Jacobs is undoubtedly correct that urban locations are where many new innovations, technologies, and forms of economic activity begin. But they need not remain in an urban environment for long after birth. Indeed, consider how manufacturing has evolved away from its initial urban environments.

In 1909, A. Weber developed an industrial location theory that stated that firms were most attracted to those "locations that minimize the total transportation costs of inputs and outputs." According to Arthur C. Nelson,

> Nineteenth-century cities were thus located where labor supply, intercity and local markets, and raw material were found nearby. Those cities were densely populated and manufacturing highly centralized.
>
> The relationships between labor, capital, material and market have changed considerably during the twentieth century. *Manufacturing has nearly abandoned the city core altogether for distant sites seemingly removed from labor, material, and markets.... Manufacturing firms have become more footloose in the latter quarter of the twentieth century than at any other time in history.*

From Arthur C. Nelson, "Regional Patterns of Exurban Patterns of Exurban Industrialization: Results of a Preliminary Investigation," *Economic Development Quarterly* 4 no.4 (November 1990): 321-322.

A. Weber's classical industrial location theory explained the reality of nineteenth century cities rather well. It certainly does not explain what Nelson called the *counterurbanization*: the emergence of the exurban landscape as the preferred sites for manufacturing firms. Agglomeration economies was the concept used for decades to explain why industrial firms would locate in or near particular clusters, but it does not explain the phenomenon that Nelson recorded. *Will the explanatory power of this concept of agglomeration economies for producer services be sustained or decline as they mature in the next decade?*

To draw the analogy tighter, Nelson has explained that the decentralization of manufacturing was facilitated by the changing technology of manufacturing processes (that is, "modern technology allows for greater substitution of labor by machines") and the declining transportation costs for freight and labor. What changes in technology or processes might alter the current urban advantages through agglomeration economics for producer services? or in other growing sectors of our economy that flourished first in urban areas? *Will the technologies of tomorrow be able to leapfrog the space that separates rural workers and the jobs of sustained prosperity in a globally competitive future?*

33. William A. Galston, "Rural America in the 1990s: Trends and Choices," *Policy Studies Journal* 20, no.2 (1992): 207.

34. The Roper Organization, Inc., *Public Attitudes toward Rural America and Rural Electric Cooperatives*, Commissioned by the National Rural Electric Cooperative Association, Washington, D.C. (1992): 27.

35. Ibid., 29.

36. C. Bell and H. Newby, *Community Studies: An Introduction to the Sociology of the Local Community* (New York: Praeger, 1972), 23 as quoted in Emilia E. Martinez-Brawley, *Perspectives on the Small Community: Humanistic View for Practitioners.* (Silver Spring, Md.: NASW Press, 1990), 5. According to Bell and Newby, "(Ferdinand) Tonnies's book *Gemeinschaft and Gesellschaft* (usually translated as Community and Society) was first published in 1887. It has provided a constant source of ideas for those who have dealt with the community ever since." See also Kai Erikson, *Everything in Its Path* (New York: Simon and Schuster, 1976).

37. Much of the academic research on rural development compares rural communities, though extremely diverse, with metropolitan areas in the aggregate. (Sometimes aggregate analysis provides a good view of the forest, but not of the trees.) In this conventional approach, many rural areas lack scale economies and other urban attributes, but they nevertheless have distinct comparative advantages such as location, lifestyle, and lower land and labor costs. But this analysis, limited to the domestic context, has less utility as global competition increases and the national economy becomes restructured.

38. See Nathan Rosenberg, *Perspectives on Technology* (Cambridge:at the University Press, 1976), 192; as quoted by W.W. Rostow, *Theorists of Economic Growth from David Hume to the Present*, (New York: Oxford University Press, 1990), 455. Here is a brief section from Rosenberg:

> …One might almost be tempted to say of James Watt that he was "just an improvere," although such a statement would be comparable to saying of Napoleon that he was just a soldier or of Bach that he was just a court musician. That is to say, Watt's improvements on the steam engine transformed it from an instrument of limited applicability at locations peculiarly favored by access to cheap fuel, to a generalized source of much wider significance.

39. Kenneth L. Deavers, "Comments," GAO Symposium on Rural Development, June 1992, as quoted in *Rural Development: Rural America Faces Many Challenges* (GAO/RCED-93-35) (Washington, D.C.: General Accounting Office, November 1992), 35.

CHAPTER 2

Rationales for Public Intervention

Cultivators of the earth are the most valuable citizens. They are the most vigorous, the most independent, the most virtuous, and they are tied to their country, and wedded to its liberty and interests, by the most lasting bonds. As long, therefore, as they can find employment in this line, I would not convert them to...anything else.   — Thomas Jefferson, (1785)[1]

Much has changed since Thomas Jefferson offered his praise for an agrarian society. Early actions of the infant federal government such as the Northwest Ordinances of 1787, which provided public land for schools and roads in newly settled territories, and the Louisiana Purchase (1803), which more than doubled the size of the nation, established what could be called the first rural development policy.

Through these and subsequent actions, the federal government facilitated frontier settlement and the expansion of the agrarian society. Efforts by Whigs and western Democrats to aid the settlement and growth of the West focused on roads, canals, and, later, railroads. The Homestead Act of 1862 provided public land to encourage the rapid settlement of the prairie and mountain West and to achieve widespread ownership of rural resources. The Morrill Act also in 1862 created the land grant universities. The national government provided public lands and generous financial support to develop railroads throughout the nation.[2]

Rural development strategies by the federal government continued to be among its major domestic priorities well into this century. Indeed, the Hatch Act of 1887 created a system of agricultural research and the Smith-Lever Act of 1914 created the extension program. The New Deal programs included the Rural Electrification Administration to bring electricity to the farms and the

Chart 2-1

A Century of Federal Programs for Rural Development

President/ Year	Rural Characteristics	Initiatives	Goals
Grover Cleveland			
1893	42% of population live on farms;	Office of Road Inquiry	Demonstration/educational
Theodore Roosevelt			
1905		Office of Public Roads	Construct roads/ tests
1908	54% live in rural areas;	Country Live Commission	Report on rural needs
Howard Taft			
1912		Office of Public roads receives funding to build rural post roads	
Woodrow Wilson			
1920	Farm population— 32 million; 30% of U.S. total;		
Warren Harding			
1921	3.2 million miles of rural roads built;		
Calvin Coolidge			
Herbert Hoover			
Franklin Roosevelt			
1933	10% of farms electrified; 26% of population live on farms;	Tennessee Valley Authority est.	
1935		Resettlement Administration	To resettle farm laborers
1936	35% of farms electrified;	Rural Electrification Adm.	To bring electricity to farms
		Cons. Farm and Rural Dev. Act	To provide business loans
1940	Farm population—30.5 million; 43% live in rural areas;		
Harry Truman			
1949	Natural resource industries produce 9% of GNP;	Rural Telephone Loan program	
1950	Farm population—25 million;		
Dwight Eisenhower			
1953		Interstate Highway System funded Small Business Act	Loans and guarantees to small businesses
1954		Housing Act	Regional planning capacity
1960	Farm population—15.6 million; Completed: 10,000 miles of Interstate and 3.1 million miles of rural roads;	Area Redev. Adm. (ARA)	Revitalize distressed rural communities

Source: Adapted from Wayne D. Rasmussen, "90 Years of *Rural Development Programs*," Rural Development Perspectives 2, no.1 (Washington, D.C.: USDA, Economic Research Service, October 1985), 6-7.

President/ Year	Rural Characteristics	Initiatives	Goals
John Kennedy			
1961		Office of Rural Area Development	To eliminate rural underemployment
1962		Rural renewal program enacted by Congress	
Lyndon Johnson			
1964		Economic Opportunity Act	To end rural poverty
		Job Corps	To train youth
1965		Housing and Urban Dev. Act	To improve housing
		Title V Regional Com.	State/Fed. partnerships on economic development
		Public Works & Econ. Dev. Act	Planning grants for rural counties/business loans
		Appalachian Regional Dev. Act	Planning grants for region
		Community Services Act	Grants to community orgs.
		Rural Com. Development Service	Coordinate USDA rural efforts
1966		National Com. on Rural Poverty	Program for attacking poverty
Richard Nixon			
1970	26% of population live in rural areas;		
1971		Rural Telephone Bank	Finance rural telephone coops
		Minority Business Centers	Tech. assistance to minority businesses
		American Indian Program	Tech. assistance to Native Americans
1972			
1974		Community Development Act	CDBG funds for rural economic and housing dev. activities
		Small Business Act	Grants to staff small business dev. centers
Jimmy Carter			
1979	99% of farms electrified;		
1980	41,000 miles of interstate highway system completed;		
Ronald Reagan			
1982	3% live on farms; 97% of farms have telephone service;		
George Bush			
1990	Natural resource industries produce 2% of GNP;	National Initiative	Est. State Rural Development Councils (SRDCs)
Bill Clinton			

Resettlement Administration to help farm laborers move to more promising locations (both in 1935), as well as a system of price supports to bolster farm incomes. The nation, according to one scholar, "invested in the basic infrastructure of agriculture, developing institutions and programs for rural free delivery of mail, rural roads, common market standards for farm products, and later for rural electrification, soil conservation, and long-term, intermediate, and short-term farm credit — all through national policy."[3]

Several themes emerge from this overview. The federal government actively promoted the development of rural areas by providing public land, building transportation systems, and creating a higher education system. In particular, the federal government during the nineteenth century aided, guided, and supervised — sometimes wisely, sometimes not — the settlement and development of the western states.[4] It provided direct services such as mail delivery, electrification, and the extension program; it created new institutions and programs. These activities reflected the broad social consensus that rural living should not be denied essential services and that the federal government had a responsibility to provide them. (Chart 2-1 presents "A Century of Federal Programs for Rural Development.")

Another noteworthy theme involves the degree to which the federal government has helped to shape agricultural policy. It promoted the broad ownership of land to encourage settlement, which reflects both Jefferson's view of the virtues of agrarian society and the early Republican philosophy of individualism and private ownership. It invested in research, education, and conservation policies to increase productivity. It sought to bolster farm incomes by providing price supports, drought relief, crop insurance, credit programs, and subsidies for certain farm exports.

A federal agricultural policy is no substitute for a national rural development policy. For most of our history, farming had been the mainstay of most rural economies. Farming continues to be very important, and much of the nation's land is used in agriculture, but it provides an ever shrinking number of jobs. In 1908, when President Theodore Roosevelt established the Country Life Commission, more than 30 percent of the population *lived on farms and a majority — 54 percent — lived in rural areas.* By 1950, 12 percent of the population lived on farms. By 1970, only 5 percent of the population lived on farms and 26 percent lived in rural areas. Today, approximately 2 percent of the nation's population lives on farms or only 9 percent of the population of nonmetropolitan counties.[5] (See chart 2-2.)

The migration of population from rural to urban areas, which began in the nineteenth century and accelerated after World War II, may be generally

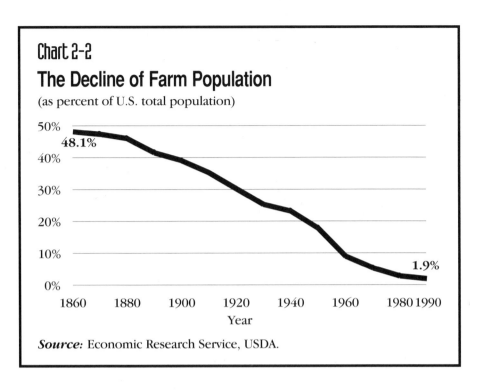

Chart 2-2
The Decline of Farm Population
(as percent of U.S. total population)

Source: Economic Research Service, USDA.

understood. Yet, paradoxically, much of the public still clings to the myths that most rural Americans are farmers and that agriculture continues to be the mainstay of most rural economies. Approximately one-fourth of our rural counties, mostly in the Midwest, are dependent upon agriculture (the standard definition of agriculture-dependent counties are those that receive more than 20 percent of their earnings from farming). But these counties account for less than 7 percent of the U.S. nonmetropolitan population. In contrast, 32 percent of the nonmetropolitan population live in manufacturing-dependent counties, which are defined as receiving 30 percent of their income from that sector.[6] The remaining half of nonmetropolitan counties receive less than 20 percent of their income from farming and less than 30 percent from manufacturing.

The popular myth that most of the rural population lives on farms has been a major obstacle to obtaining public support for economic development strategies for rural areas. A 1992 textbook, *Rural Communities: Legacy and Change*, concluded that:

> Farm programs receive nearly half of the nonentitlement funds going to rural areas. Although there is increased emphasis on comprehensive rural

development, agricultural support in the form of farm subsidies still dominates federal spending on rural development. In 1987, for example, $29 billion was spent on development programs for all of rural America; an additional $22.4 billion was spent on agricultural price and income support alone.[7]

If the general public believes that the federal agricultural subsidies and price supports provide substantial benefits to many residents of rural America, it is mistaken. This notion is no longer accurate, and probably has not been for many decades. Agriculture is no longer the primary generator of rural employment. Furthermore, analysts of federal agricultural programs have noted that these benefits flow to a rather small group of direct beneficiaries, which has motivated some observers to conclude that "farm policy should be taken for what it is, namely, (an) industrial policy with some economic benefits for farmers and their industrial partners." [8]

Employment in rural areas is surprisingly similar, in terms of standard industry categories, to the national figures. Two-thirds of the jobs in nonmetropolitan counties in 1987 were in the service sector: retail and wholesale trade, hotel and tourist operations, financial, health, legal, and government services. Manufacturing employed one in six rural workers, similar to the national average. Fewer than 10 percent work in agriculture. The debate on national rural development policy should not be confused with the equally important topic of federal agricultural policy.

The Rural Problem Restated

According to the 1990 census, less than 25 percent of the nation's population resides in rural areas. With the exception of the 1970s, nonmetropolitan counties have lost population throughout this century. More than 1,240 rural counties — over half of all rural counties — lost population during the 1980s. They lost more than 6 percent of their population — a total of 1.6 million people.[9]

Rural areas are remarkably diverse in demography, typography, economies, and cultures; what most of them have in common is geographic isolation, poor infrastructure and limited fiscal capacity. Compared with metropolitan counties, according to a 1992 study, rural communities "have higher rates of poverty, unemployment, and mortality; lower levels of educational attainment, employment skills, and vocational training; and more limited access to health care, social services, public water systems, and a modern telecommunication system." [10]

Rural advocates have sought a comprehensive rural development policy and an adequate level of federal resources based on both the history of the federal government's rich involvement in developing its rural areas and the *moral claim* that the federal government is responsible for improving the quality of life in existing places. Fenton Johnson, a native of Kentucky who has written about the economic depression of Appalachian coal towns, expressed this moral claim when he challenged proposed government relocation programs to move the rural population to more prosperous cities. In 1992, he wrote that:

> The relocation policy implies giving up not just on eastern Kentucky but on whole regions of the world — in America, parts of the Great Plains and the rural South come to mind. These are places where cultures once flourished, that are now being depopulated to the verge of extinction. At a time when capitalism and democracy are seen as triumphant worldwide, for a whole region of America to slide into a depopulated environmental wasteland represents an unnerving failure, at least of capitalism, perhaps — in its betrayal of its citizens — of democracy itself.[11]

Another articulate voice for this moral claim has come from Osha Gray Davidson in his book, *Broken Heartland: The Rise of America's Rural Ghetto:*

> In rural America, we are now making the terrible (and yet wholly logical) leap from marginalizing individuals to marginalizing whole communities, and perhaps even to rendering an entire region superfluous to the flow of American life. As politicians profess a deep and abiding love of "Heartland values," thousands of small towns spread out across the American countryside are left to wither on the vine.[12]

The moral claim is intertwined with the history of the federal government's long involvement in shaping rural development. Quite apart from this history, however, the moral claim still resonates: regardless of where we live, most of us feel that it is *our* federal government and that it should ensure the provision of essential public services. The moral claim has been made strongly by political leaders and advocates in the western states because the federal government owns and manages such vast holdings of public lands. Because it controls as much as 80 percent of the land in some of the western states, federal natural resource management policies exert a vital impact upon the viability of rural development throughout the West.

Related to the moral claim that the federal government is responsible for improving the quality of life in existing places is the argument for giving special attention to rural areas *to improve rural-urban equity*. As discussed, nonmetropolitan counties have higher rates of poverty and unemployment than metropolitan counties. Employment growth has been slower in rural counties, and population declined during the 1980s. Average family wages are lower in rural counties than in urban counties, and this wage disparity increased during the 1980s.

Of particular concern is the growing disparity of metro and nonmetro earnings across various educational attainment levels. For example, in 1974 individuals with an eighth grade education earned a dollar and eight cents in the metro counties compared with every one dollar earned by the same group in the nonmetro counties. This earnings penalty increased by 1986 when the metro-nonmetro earnings ratio rose from 1.08 to 1.18; the metro-nonmetro earnings ratio for college graduates rose from 1.14 in 1974 to 1.40 in 1986. The earnings penalty at different education levels suggests that a narrower range of employment opportunities is available in rural as compared with urban counties, which is one reason that so many college-educated young people have moved from their rural homes to urban areas.[13]

Another equity argument also merits attention. Rural advocates and urban planners have long lamented that various federal programs stimulated development in suburban areas in the decades following the end of World War II. They contend that both inner city neighborhoods and rural communities were disadvantaged by federal highway and housing programs that fostered suburban development. Hence, they have argued that this implicit federal growth policy, which for decades sent billions of dollars to aid suburban development, now justifies substantial, compensating federal appropriations to both rural and urban communities.

Each of these arguments is important: the historical federal role in rural development, the moral claim that government has a responsibility to ensure that essential services are provided throughout the nation, the appeal for special assistance to rural areas to improve rural-urban equity, and the call for compensation owing to the geographic distortions aided and abetted by past federal programs. Neither passionate rhetoric nor sober arguments, though, have been effective in shifting public resources toward rural America. A partial explanation for this is found in box 2-1.

Box 2-1
Obstacles to a National Rural Development Policy

Altering the minimalist rural development policy of the past will be a formidable task. The dilemma, as Louis Swanson has pointed out, has at least five dimensions. The first is the myth that the fortunes of the farm sector determine those of the rural area — hence farm policy is a viable surrogate for rural development. Then, social, economic, demographic, and other types of information on rural areas is woefully limited and even misleading.

In addition, there is a pervasive assumption, very much associated with the current triage policy, that little can be done to help rural areas left behind. The odd corollary is that these areas will not pose much of a problem for the nation, given their isolation from the national economy. Will their people, their problems, and their ability to touch the rest of society simply disappear?

Then, rural areas are often treated in isolation from larger regional, national, and international economies. The interconnectedness of rural issues with policy issues in other areas is frequently overlooked. For example, nonmetropolitan and metro central city counties are remarkably similar in terms of poverty, unemployment, crime, and other socio-economic indicators.

The final dilemma is a lack of unified national constituency. Very few interests are organized at the national level to support rural development, but there are some impressively organized groups that work as obstacles. Among these are the major farm and agricultural commodities groups, who probably correctly see monies for rural development as eventually coming from farm price-support policy.

Source: William P. Browne, Jerry R. Skees, Louis E. Swanson, Paul B. Thompson, and Laurian J. Unnevehr, *Sacred Cows and Hot Potatoes: Agrarian Myths in Agricultural Policy*, (Boulder, Colo.: Westview Press, 1992), 33-34.[14]

Who Cares about Rural America?

The residents of rural communities, and their elected officials, care deeply about the economic viability of their communities. Most state officials share this concern and many are searching for appropriate economic development strategies for these areas. But who else shares these concerns? Why should urban and suburban residents care about the economic fate of rural America? Indeed, if economic development strategies for rural communities require substantial public resources, would urban and suburban taxpayers be willing to support these expenditures?

Is the viability of rural economies a national concern? The 1990 census revealed that more than three-quarters of the U.S. population now resides in the country's 284 metropolitan areas (almost half in suburbs and more than thirty percent in cities). This demography suggests that a national policy requiring substantial public resources to enhance rural economies may encounter major opposition — even if a compelling rationale is articulated and a sophisticated political strategy is devised.

Despite the veil of sympathetic rhetoric by congressmen, cabinet secretaries, and presidents about the future of rural America, federal resources directed to rural communities have been declining. The retrenchment of federal policy toward all communities, as evidenced by reduced grants to state and local governments, also reveals a clear movement away from federal place-oriented strategies.

Several of the domestic programs created during the New Deal and the Great Society eras established an expanded federal role in place-oriented policies: the Tennessee Valley Authority, the Appalachian Regional Commission, and various grants-in-aid programs for local governments. Yet, during the past two decades, federal resources to states and localities have gradually declined, and there have been no new major federal programs to pursue what might be called place-oriented strategies. (It is debatable whether the Intermodal Surface Transportation Efficiency Act of 1991, which authorized increased federal funds to state and local governments, constitutes the single exception; it has not yet been fully funded.) With this fiscal retrenchment and the loss of federal resources, increasing responsibilities have been assumed by the states and their communities.

The public rhetoric about preserving places — "Why yes, of course" — far exceeds the actual allocation of federal resources devoted to this social objective. During the last four national administrations, the federal government has diminished its funding for programs to preserve existing places. Has the public lost faith in this principle as well? The overriding trend of federal budget expenditures during this period has been toward national programs directed to benefit people — not places.

One of the arguments justifying the federal disengagement from place-oriented strategies might be called the rational choice argument, which begins with the observation that residents of rural communities are making personal choices about where they live. If rural residents are willing to bear the associated sacrifices in terms of lower incomes, fewer job opportunities, or meager public services from living in rural areas, then, according to this view, they may be placing a higher personal value on living with a low incidence of crime, the aesthetics of the countryside, and the quality of life and civic virtues of small town America.[15] Why invest public resources to improve economically depressed places when the residents are free to move elsewhere but prefer to stay? America is the land of opportunity and, if rural areas have insufficient opportunity, according to this view, then why not have the residents move to where the jobs and opportunities are? The rational choice argument cannot be dismissed casually.

As discussed, mobility and opportunity are important historical themes for our nation. People initially perceived personal opportunities through settling in rural areas and then they chose to migrate from them. Approximately ten million people left farms between 1920 and 1940 and another thirty-one million migrated from farms between 1940 and 1978.[16] Caught between the push from technological improvements in agriculture that eliminated traditional employment and the pull of higher paying jobs in the growing industrial centers of the country, they clearly made personal choices, often bittersweet ones, about where to pursue the prospect of employment and social opportunities. Similarly, the continued movement of retirees into rural communities during the 1970s and 1980s also reflects the rational choices of many within our society who have chosen to move to pursue personal objectives. Perhaps the highly mobile nature of our society partly explains the public's ambivalence toward place-oriented government programs.

In addition, most economists contend that efforts to improve labor mobility to locations with expanding employment opportunities would be a superior public policy compared with providing government subsidies to stimulate growth in chronically depressed areas. This recommendation has been called a *transition policy* because it proposes to assist people who lack the means to relocate to areas with expanded employment opportunity and to help prepare them for available jobs.[17] Yet, without public intervention, these depressed areas — including both stagnant rural communities and innercity neighborhoods — would continue to deteriorate.

Robert Reich framed the policy choice in this way:

> What should be done to help rural America? One view is that we should do
> nothing. For generations, Americans have been leaving farms and small
> towns, bound for cities…. By this view, it makes sense to help someone gain
> new skills and relocate where good jobs are available, but not to pour
> money into particular communities or regions in hopes of attracting or
> keeping industries there. The first alternative improves the nation's efficien-
> cy by shifting human resources to where they can be put to their best use;
> the second is inefficient, because it keeps people and industries in places —
> and doing things — where the costs of production are just too high.[18]

The increasing support for transition policies during the last two decades
appears to have been associated with a decline in public support for place-
enhancing strategies. A significant milestone came in late 1980 when President
Carter's Commission for a National Agenda for the Eighties issued its final
report. This commission observed soberly that "Contrary to conventional
wisdom, cities are not permanent…we forget that cities, like all living things,
change." The commission advocated the shift from urban policy to social policy
— a federal strategy of funding the needs of people instead of places.[19]

The initial hostile reaction of this report came from urban advocates, city
planners, and others who believed that the federal government must continue
to exert a primary responsibility to assist cities. At the time, though, few rural
advocates realized the broader policy implication: that the federal government
disengage from its prior responsibility to assist existing places. The report
proved to be prescient, however, because national policy during the following
twelve years clearly deemphasized place-oriented federal programs.

Valiantly swimming against the tide, mayors, urban advocates, and academics continued during the 1980s to assert that cities were nationally important and continued to deserve special federal assistance. Big city mayors convened from time to time to proclaim the importance of federal programs to aid
the cities, but these pleas have not resonated among the increasing number of
voters who no longer live or work in the larger cities. Even some of the strongest advocates for placing cities at the top of the national agenda during the
1970s and 1980s have recently counseled that "renewed efforts to establish a
national urban policy" would be futile.[20]

Another example of this view comes from one of the better critiques of the
enterprise zone concept, which proposed — instead of trying to lure jobs to
these depressed areas with special tax incentives — that special programs be

developed to relocate or transport the residents of depressed communities to those areas with high job growth. The author, John D. Kasarda, a University of North Carolina professor of Business Administration and Sociology, concluded this critique with the observation that "It is not fortuitous that the three great symbols of social and economic opportunity of America's disadvantaged all relate to spatial mobility — the Statue of Liberty, the underground railway, and the covered wagon."[21]

The logic of this policy prescription — that policymakers should not invest public funds into preserving places, but rather assist people to move to areas with more opportunities — has a certain appeal in the abstract, particularly to those in academia or to those far removed from the responsibility of making policy choices affecting economically depressed communities. Economists who recommend a transition policy that responds to declining rural economies by helping the underemployed or unemployed to migrate to growing urban areas provide little comfort to state policymakers whose responsibility it is to devise strategic economic development policies and programs.

If the public is skeptical about a clearly defined or coherent national urban policy and generally has less faith in place-oriented strategies, would it support a national rural policy? Is a modest degree of optimism justified? Here are the traditional arguments:

The history of federal involvement in rural development is long and distinguished (unlike the short-lived urban policy). But will the pull of history be effective in Congress?

The federal government has a responsibility to ensure that all citizens, regardless of where they live, receive essential public services. But how strongly does the public share this conviction? Which public services are essential?

A majority of the public continues to support federal agricultural programs — probably treating it as a surrogate for rural policy. In the late 1980s, public opinion polls revealed that two of every three U.S. citizens supported farm programs.[22] But how does public opinion register on the scale of congressional votes? Unlike agricultural interests, rural advocates have neither strong articulate trade groups nor lobbyists.

The public living and working in metropolitan America — representing more than 75 percent of the national population — is fond of both rural

Americans and rural America, as places. Does this fondness reflect strong support for federal interventions? What does the public know about rural America or its problems?

The 1992 Roper survey for the National Rural Electric Cooperative Association produced a summary that provides some insight into these questions:

> Americans continue to have an enduring admiration for rural Americans. Rural Americans continue to be thought of as family oriented, friendly, honest, responsible, religious, and less stressed than their urban counterparts. *Another enduring impression is that urban and suburban problems do not affect rural America or constitute an important threat.... The public still does not recognize or think about the poverty and social problems prevalent in rural America.* Rural America itself may have changed but the way in which most Americans view it has not. In the eyes of most Americans, rural America has an embarrassment of riches, not problems. (Emphasis added.)[23]

According to these findings, the public romanticizes rural America; it does not understand that much of rural America has special needs that merit attention. Indeed, one astute observer noted that the above summary could well have described how we feel about our national parks. Will this idealized perception of rural Americans lead urban visitors to view them as mere stagehands who appear at scenic vistas and tourist attractions to serve their needs?[24]

One would hope that there would be greater support for federal intervention to aid rural development if the public knew that there is a higher poverty rate, a higher unemployment rate, a higher percentage of inadequate housing, and a higher percentage of people over the age of 65 in rural America than in the nations' cities.[25] Rural advocates can enrich the public debate by emphasizing a more realistic assessment of the challenges and strengths of rural America.

Even if the above obstacles can be overcome and the federal government spends more in the future to preserve or improve existing places, would rural communities then receive sufficient resources from this policy shift? The problems of the inner city historically have received more attention from national political leaders than the problems of rural areas. To paraphrase one member of Congress who spoke soon after the Los Angeles riot in the spring of 1992: "The alienated and discontented of urban areas sometimes cause riots, but the alienated and discontented in rural areas have never rioted."[26]

As much as one might hope that the federal government will reassert its role in preserving places, the final obstacle is demographic — the majority of this nation's voters now live in suburban areas. How might they be convinced that targeting more federal resources to aid rural communities (or, big cities, or both) is a policy they should support? Could a broad coalition between rural and urban advocates be formed to press for renewed federal resources for targeted place-oriented programs? Could these place-oriented advocates develop a compelling rationale for these policies that the general public supports? Will the federal government reassert its historic role in developing place-oriented programs? And if it does, would this be sufficient to make rural economies competitive in our information-dominated society or in competitive global markets?[27]

The Rationale for State Intervention

Rural advocates and community leaders increasingly have directed their concerns and attention at state governments that bear the *dual responsibilities* of preserving their places and of providing benefits to their citizens.[28] Declining federal resources allocated to meet the pressing needs of rural communities have forced many leaders to make more claims on state governments. In addition, state governments have economic, social, and political interests in assuring that their rural economies are healthy and provide a range of employment and business opportunities.

During the past two decades, states have developed various economic development strategies and programs to improve their overall states' performance. They continue to emphasize industrial recruitment and retention, but states also have developed new initiatives to assist small business development, have devised new financing programs, have invested in technology development, and have experimented with various organizational designs to provide business assistance.[29] (Chapter 3 presents a summary of these programs and, in that context, chapter 4 presents an overview of various economic development strategies to improve rural competitiveness.)

In addition to the self-interested political arguments for state intervention in assisting rural economies, several different equity arguments have also been used. Although it may be rhetorically advantageous for rural advocates to demand that state government assure *equity of outcomes* across all regions within a state, this may not be a realistic equity standard because state governments have neither sufficient resources to guide economic development activities nor the authority to direct private sector investment decisions.

Another equity standard, sometimes called *vertical equity*, would maintain that the special needs of rural communities require special state programs and development assistance. School districts, for example, provide special teachers and programs for those children with special needs or learning disabilities. Chronic rural poverty should merit a special claim on the resources of state government, especially its economic development programs. Other characteristics of rural communities — low population density, isolation, lower job skill levels, poor infrastructure, more elderly, greater poverty, and poorly financed schools — could justify special assistance by state governments. Indeed, compared with those of most metropolitan counties, rural economies have significant infrastructure needs, weaker fiscal capacity from which to provide basic public services, and less organizational capacity with which to develop and implement self-help strategies. *This constitutes the major equity claim on state resources for special economic development assistance.*

Two less rigorous standards for state governments would be to assure that *equal efforts* are being made to further the interests of rural economies or that *equal benefits* are being received by rural communities. Objective documentation indicating that essential state programs and services have not been distributed equitably to rural communities may be effective in policy deliberations at the state level to achieve greater distributional equity.

The implicit argument is that some form of public intervention should seek to achieve relative equity between rural and urban areas within a state in terms of broad social conditions. How much should be attempted by state government to achieve relative equity in terms of family income or employment opportunities is likely to be a continuing controversy; it is a political question. It may surface as a campaign issue if the media or public attention is given to rural-urban equity concerns. Or, this issue could be ignored by the public yet remain a prominent battleground for state legislators. It is, nevertheless, addressed — either explicitly or implicitly — each time a state budget is proposed by the governor and subsequently adopted by the legislature.

Critics of providing special assistance to rural communities are likely to note that, at best, state government can only marginally guide development activities. It may be accurate that many existing economic development programs have generated rather modest benefits, but this does not explain why those benefits should be disproportionately enjoyed by urban or suburban communities (if, indeed, that does occur). As state policymakers expand their concept of economic development policy to include the provision of essential public services — education, physical infrastructure, job training, and community development — then it becomes readily apparent that many rural communities will require special assistance from their state governments. As discussed, how to allocate or whether to ration these state resources are decisions that rest with the governors and state legislatures.

Efficiency Arguments

Efficiency gains or social benefits might accrue to the public from state investments in assisting the competitiveness of rural economies. Successful initiatives to improve rural incomes and employment opportunities, if not implemented at the expense of other jurisdictions, would add to our national wealth. Some economists have asserted that various market failures have caused the underperformance of rural economies and provide the rationale for public intervention. (See box 2-2 for an excerpt on this concept.) Public intervention, therefore, would be justified in such situations in addressing these market failures, which would improve efficiencies and increase aggregate output with the same level of inputs.

Economists may not agree, naturally, on whether a market failure exists. At least one prominent expert in the field of rural development has suggested "that, beyond information shortages, there is no strong evidence of substantial across-the-board market failures in rural America."[30] In addition, even some of the economists who acknowledge the existence of specific market failures have argued vehemently that most forms of public intervention would be either ineffective, inefficient, or both — hence, worse than no intervention at all.

Other Social Objectives

Stimulating economic growth in rural areas that have existing physical infrastructure (such as schools, roads, municipal water and sewage systems, and other public facilities) is often a rational state planning objective. The adverse effects caused by rapid urban growth in many regions of the country have led many to question the associated social and financial costs of urban expansion. Higher local taxes, increased traffic congestion, more air pollution, over-crowded highways, and other negative by-products of uncontrolled urban growth have forced more attention on maintaining quality-of-life objectives. Hence, the balanced or managed growth advocates have joined forces with rural community leaders to search for land use regulations and other policy options that might shift future regional growth toward rural communities.[31]

Box 2-2
Efficiency Arguments for
Regional Economic Development Policy

In a 1991 article, Timothy J. Bartik argued that regional economic development policies should aim to correct failures of private markets to achieve greater efficiency. He defines the following private market failures as conditions that could provide the rationale for public intervention to improve efficiency:

Unemployment, when "individuals without employment are willing to work at the prevailing wage for jobs for which they are qualified.... Reducing involuntary employment for current residents is a nonmarket benefit that is a possible goal to be maximized by regional economic development policy."

Underemployment, when the existence of sizable wage differences across industries "cannot be explained by differences in workers' skills. Shifting a regional economy toward high-wage premium industries provides nonmarket benefits that are a possible goal of regional economic development policy."

Human capital, when "individuals underinvest.... There are four possible reasons for underinvestment in human capital. First, individuals may have difficulty financing training or education because lenders cannot repossess human capital. Second, education may increase social stability by instilling civic virtues or by providing a sense of opportunity for the poor. Third, human capital may have externality benefits, because one worker's ideas enhance the creativity of other workers. Fourth, human capital's value is hard to measure before acquisition."

Robert Reich suggested in the mid-1980s that one justification for public intervention to revitalize rural economies was:

> ...the social costs of crowding. Many of our coastal areas are becoming overcrowded and overbuilt — facing mounting problems of pollution, inadequate housing, overtaxed disposal facilities, traffic congestion, and unsafe spaces for children to play. There is a social value to dispersing our

Research and innovation spillovers, when businesses and individuals do not consider social gains (from new product or production techniques adopted by others), but rather "only their own private gain, thus leading to underinvestment in research, development, and innovation…. The innovation spillover argument may justify economic development programs that subsidize applied research (e.g., Pennsylvania's Ben Franklin Partnership Program) or product development (e.g., the Connecticut Product Development Corporation)."

Other imperfections in information markets, when "underprovided by private markets…. The problems with private information provision may rationalize government programs that provide information intended to encourage economic development; industrial extension services that provide information on modernization, expert information programs; and marketing programs providing information on potential new branch plant sites."

Imperfect capital markets, whenever " socially profitable loans or investments are not made. There are three possible causes of such market failures. First, financial markets in the U.S. are regulated. Competition among banks is restricted, and this may limit credit availability. Furthermore, risks taken by financial institutions are supposedly restricted by government regulation. This may prevent financial institutions from making risky loans or investments despite an expected good return."

Source: Timothy J. Bartik, "The Market Failure Approach to Regional Economic Development Policy" Economic Development Quarterly 4 no.4, (November 1990): 361-370.

population across the land. That's why all of us urban dwellers have a long-term stake in an economically sound rural America.[32]

This argument has also been advanced in a less elegant way. Urban constituencies should be willing, according to this view, to support increased economic stimulus for rural communities to stabilize employment opportunities for rural residents, thereby reducing the migration to the cities and slowing future urban growth. But this message has a crude undertone as well: the failure to do this would cause rural residents, with all of their assorted problems, to flood the cities in search of employment — destroying the quality of urban life in the process.[33] Enlightened self-interest should, therefore, encourage urban and suburban taxpayers to support special initiatives to promote viable rural economies.

Urban dwellers may also have an economic stake in the viability of surrounding rural communities. Continued rural economic stagnation could drain away urban-generated tax dollars. Vibrant, healthy rural economies, in contrast, enhance the vitality of regional urban centers. Improving rural-urban linkages can strengthen both components of an economic region. Several academics, for example, have estimated that very large proportions of the gross product of regional urban centers are generated by economic activity outside those urban areas. Their work clearly demonstrates that healthy rural economies should be among the concerns of urban residents.[34]

What is the value to metropolitan residents of being able to enjoy the countryside and an adequate level of public services during their stay while on recreational jaunts, ski trips, vacations, and family visits? Several economists, for example, interpret the high level of agricultural subsidies provided within the European Common Market as an explicit social payment for the maintenance of aesthetically pleasing greenbelts between their cities. Could similar arguments be advanced: that state resources should be directed toward improving the quality of life in rural areas both for the benefit of those who live there and for the benefit of others who use them for recreation, escape, and relaxation? This is yet another way of articulating the urban self-interest in maintaining viable rural economies.

Rural property owners and managers, it has been argued, should be serving the public's interest by conserving, preserving, and protecting many of our national resources. The concept of a stewardship of natural resources exceeds meeting government regulations and rising public expectations for environmental protection. For some years, "sustainable development" has become a popular phrase; it means that future prosperity depends on preserving and investing in "natural capital" — air, water, and other ecological resources — and that doing so will require balancing human activity with nature's ability to renew itself. It recognizes that growth is necessary to eliminate poverty, but emphasizes the importance of finding ways to satisfy present needs without jeopardizing the prospects of future generations.[35]

Although this concept was first articulated as an argument to assist the less developed nations in stimulating economic growth to avoid exploiting their natural environments, the concept also has value for those thinking about the economic and environmental prospects of rural America. Simply put, the failure to invest in rural economies invites the exploitation of natural resources. Environmentalists seeking to preserve species, forests, mountains, lakes, wetlands, or other unique locations throughout the nation must also acknowledge and accept the responsibility for assisting with alternative (and sustainable) economic development activities for these rural communities.[36] Residents of rural America should not be asked to serve, informally and unofficially, as the stewards of the nation's natural resources, if in doing so they are denied minimal business and employment opportunities.

Summary

Ours is a pluralistic society in which any group can assert its claim — regardless of merit — for special tax privileges, subsidies, loans, or grants from the public sector. Usually these claims are adorned with justifications that emphasize equity concerns or efficiency promises. "It is only fair," for example, "that all children attending public schools within a state receive the same level of resources," or, "A cut in capital gains taxes will boost the national economy." The people we elect to public office face the unenviable chore of sorting out these diverse and competing claims.

Rural advocates must advance more sophisticated arguments for public intervention to aid rural economies than simply appealing for basic fairness. Well-developed equity and efficiency arguments will be necessary to convince both the public and policymakers that rural economies merit special attention. Our agrarian history and the nostalgia for the virtuous rural life are apparently not sufficiently compelling reasons to motivate public support to invest in aiding our rural economies. Nor is it clear that arguing for the self-interest of the metropolitan public will be successful, either.

This nation has a long history of federal assistance in rural development. Recently, however, the domestic policy focus has shifted from being partly place-oriented to being predominantly people-oriented. Although federal agricultural programs have retained the attention and commitment of policymakers, the few recent national rural development initiatives have been feeble. Is it realistic to hope that the federal government will reassert its role in preserving existing places? Tempering one's optimism is the political dominance of suburban voters, who may be less willing to support such national policies, as well as the chorus of economists who recommend the transitional approach to rural development.

States have emerged during the 1980s as the leaders in designing innovative economic development strategies and programs, which are summarized in chapter 3. The challenge of formulating effective strategies to promote rural competitiveness, which are discussed in chapter 4, is likely to confront the states.

Notes:

1. Saul K. Padover, *Thomas Jefferson on Democracy*, (Mentor, 1939), 68 (from a letter Jefferson sent to John Jay) as quoted in "The Rural Economic Policy Choice," *Rural America in Transition*, ed. Mark Drabenstott and Lynn Gibson, (Kansas City: Federal Reserve Bank of Kansas City, 1988), 72.

2. See Richard White, *It's Your Misfortune and None of My Own: A New History of the American West* (Norman, Okla.: University of Oklahoma Press, 1991), especially Part II; also see Drabenstott, Henry, and Gibson, *Rural America In Transition*, 59-84; James T. Bonnen, "Why is There No Coherent U.S. Rural Policy?" *Policy Studies Journal* 20, no.2 (1992): 190-201; and Cornelia Butler Flora, Jan I. Flora, Jacqueline D. Spears, Louis E. Swanson with Mark B. Lapping and Mark K. Weinberg *Rural Communities: Legacy and Change* (Boulder, Colo.: Westview Press, 1992).

3. Bonnen "U.S. Rural Policy," 190.

4. See Richard White, *"It's Your Misfortune"* Part II.

5. Wayne D. Rasmussen, "90 Years of Rural Development Programs," *Rural Development Perspectives* 2, no. 1, (1985): 2-9.

6. See Bonnen (1992); and William P. Browne, Jerry R. Skees, Louis E. Swanson, Paul B. Thompson and Laurian J. Unnevehr, *Sacred Cows and Hot Potatoes: Agrarian Myths in Agricultural Policy* (Boulder, Colo.: Westview Press, 1992).

7. Flora et al. *Rural Communities*, 197.

8. According to Browne et al. *Sacred Cows*, "73 percent of farm program benefits go to only 15 percent of the largest farms." p.45. Text quote from page 35.

9. Richard L. Deavers, "1980's A Decade of Broad Rural Stress," *Rural Development Perspectives* 7, no. 3 (June-September 1991): 5.

10. James A. Christenson and Cornelia B. Flora eds., "A Rural Policy Agenda for the 1990s," *Rural Policies for the 1990s* (Boulder, Colo.: Westview Press, 1992), 333.

11. Fenton Johnson, "In the Fields of King Coal," *New York Times Magazine*, 22 November 1992, Sec. 6, p.36.

12. Osha Gray Davidson, *Broken Heartland: The Rise of America's Rural Ghetto* (New York: Anchor Books/Doubleday, 1990), 68.

13. Deavers, "Broad Rural Stress"; See also J. Norman Reid, *Rural America: Economic Performance, 1989* (Washington, D.C.: Economic Research Service, 1989), 12: "A large percentage of adults with high school educations or less live in nonmetro areas.... These skills leave rural workers ill-prepared for the modern economy. Most new jobs created during the 1980's demanded higher levels of education. At the same time, little growth in new jobs occurred in rural areas at

any education level…. The inability of the rural economy to add high skill jobs creates strong pressures for the educated to leave rural areas."

14. See also Bonnen "U.S. Rural Policy," and Louis E. Swanson, "The Rural Development Dilemma," *Resources* 96 (Summer 1989): 14-17.

15. Many economists have made this argument; Milton Friedman is among the most prominent. It was also reflected in Ronald Reagan's pronouncement during his unsuccessful bid for the presidency in 1976 that "people should vote with their feet," if they were dissatisfied with the public services of their state. For a recent application of this analytical approach to a public policy issue, see Paul E. Peterson and Mark C. Rom, *Welfare Magnets: A New Case for a National Standard* (Washington, D.C.: Brookings, 1990) which argues that states with higher welfare benefits have acted as magnets in attracting poor people who would not otherwise move there or stay there.

16. Bonnen "U.S. Rural Policy," 191.

17. For a thoughtful discussion on transition policy, see Mark Drabenstott, Presentation at GAO Symposium on *Rural Development, Rural Development: Rural America Faces Many Challenges* GAO/RCED-93-35 (Washington, D.C.: General Accounting Office, November 1992), 49-53. According to Drabenstott (p.51): "Job one for rural policy should have been to help rural displaced workers adjust…. A second element of transition policy is to reform public services. We have problems delivering public services in many rural areas simply because of small scale. What innovative ways can we develop to encourage more efficient delivery of public services?…. A third element of transition policy is rethinking rural infrastructure. There are broad stretches of rural America where we have a serious problem funding infrastructure. We also have a problem in that we may still be thinking about physical infrastructure and not information infrastructure. Where do we make the investments and in what types of infrastructure? These are very difficult questions on which rural communities and state policy leaders need a lot of help."

18. Robert B. Reich, "The Rural Crisis, and What to Do About It," *Economic Development Quarterly* 2, no. 1, (1988): 4.

19. See President's Commission for a National Agenda for the Eighties, *Report* (Washington, D.C.: U.S. Government Printing Office, 1980), 65-67; and Robert C. Wood, "People Versus Places: The Dream Will Never Die," *Economic Development Quarterly* 5, no.2 (May 1991): 100.

20. Wood, 100; and see also Marshall Kaplan and Franklin James, eds., *The Future of National Urban Policy* (Durham, N.C.: Duke University Press, 1990).

21. John D. Kasarda, "City Jobs and Residents on a Collision Course: The Urban Underclass Dilemma" *Economic Development Quarterly* 4 no.4, (November 1990): 313-319.

22. Drabenstott, Henry, and Gibson, *Rural America in Transition*, 82.

23. Roper Organization, Inc., "Public Attitudes toward Rural America and Rural Electric Cooperatives," Commissioned by the National Rural Electric Cooperative Association, Washington, D.C. (1992): 30-31.

24. The author thanks Richard Silkman for this insight.

25. Roper Organization, Inc., "Public Attitudes," 29; also see *State of the Nation's Housing* (Cambridge, Mass.: MIT 1991).

26. At a symposium on Rural Development organized by the General Accounting Office in May 1992, soon after the Los Angeles riot, Congressman E. "KiKa" de la Garza asked rhetorically, according to the author's notes: "When was the last time you heard of a riot in a rural community? People in rural areas need jobs, too, but do you think a crowd of unemployed men would go over to the village store to riot?" An edited version of his remarks, as well as the presentations from many leading scholars in the field of rural development, appear in *Rural Development: Rural America Faces Many Challenges*, (Washington, D.C.: General Accounting Office, 1992).

27. Some may believe that the Clinton administration will reassert the federal role in improving the quality of life in existing communities. Prominent obstacles on the immediate policy landscape may temper one's optimism. They include the immediate priority of stimulating the economy out of its lethargy, the major health care reforms, the mounting federal deficits that will constrain new domestic initiatives, and the long list of policy commitments by the new president (most of which, significantly, are people-based programs).

28. This section benefits from the arguments developed in David W. Sears, John M. Redman, Richard L. Gardner, and Stephen J. Adams, *Gearing Up for Success: Organizing a State for Rural Development* (Washington, D.C.: the Aspen Institute, 1992), especially pages 51-54.

29. See Peter K. Eisinger, *The Rise of the Entrepreneurial State: State and Local Economic Development Policy in the United States* (Madison, Wis.: University of Wisconsin Press, 1988); R. Scott Fosler, ed., *The New Economic Role of American States: Strategies in a Competitive World Economy* (New York: Oxford University Press, 1988); and David Osborne, *Laboratories of Democracy: A New Breed of Governor Creates Models for National Growth* (Boston: Harvard Business School Press, 1988).

30. David W. Sears, et al., *Gearing Up for Success*, 54. See also Kenneth L. Deavers "Rural Vision—Rural Reality: Efficiency, Equity, Public Goods, and the Future of Rural Policy," *Benjamin H. Hibbard Memorial Lecture Series* (Madison, Wisconsin: Department of Agricultural Economics, University of Wisconsin, April 20, 1990).

31. One of the best sources of information about growth management issues is the Lincoln Institute of Land Policy, 113 Brattle Street, Cambridge, Mass. 02138-3400; 617.661.3016. See also John DeGrove with the assistance of Deborah A. Miness, *The New Frontier for Land Policy: Planning and Growth Management in the States* (Cambridge, Mass.: Lincoln Institute of Land Policy, 1992).

32. Robert B. Reich, "The Rural Crisis, and What to Do About It," *Economic Development Quarterly* 2 no.1, (1988): 5.

33. See Johnson, "In the Fields of King Coal," *New York Times Magazine*, (1992), p.36, who quotes Tom Miller, a program officer at the Ford Foundation and a former president of Kentucky Highlands: "In more isolated counties the people leaving are those with the most resources and ambition. And when those people leave they often carry their troubles to the place they move to. That cost to society provides a fiscal as well as human compassion reason to develop the region."

34. The author wishes to thank Richard Gardner for patiently explaining the significance of this observation. For a discussion of regional economic linkages, see David Harrison and Jonathan Seib, "Toward One Region: Strengthening Rural-Urban Economic Linkages," *A Northwest Reader: Options for Rural Communities* (Seattle, Wash.: Northwest Policy Center, 1989). For a sample of the fine work done by natural resource economists, see M. Henry Robison, Neil L. Meyer, and

Roger Coupal, *The Role of Rural Industry in Idaho's Urban Places* (Moscow, Idaho: University of Idaho Cooperative Extension, October 1992); to wit from page one:

> In southeastern Idaho, fully 56 percent of urban Rexburg-Idaho Falls-Pocatello's gross product is generated by economic activity outside the urban area....

> In southwestern Idaho, 31 percent of urban Boise-Nampa-Caldwell's gross product is generated by economic activity outside the urban place....

35. See Stephan Schmidheiny with the Business Council for Sustainable Development, *Changing Course: A Global Business Perspective on Development and the Environment* (Cambridge, Mass.: MIT Press, 1992).

36. Kirk Johnson, "Environmentalism and the Challenge of Sustainable Development" in *The Changing Northwest* (Seattle, Washington: Northwest Policy Center, June-July 1991).

CHAPTER 3

State Economic Development Policies and Rural Competitiveness

§ tates have become leaders in confronting the global challenge to American competitiveness. Considered by some people to be Constitutional anachronisms not too many years ago, states have reasserted their traditional roles as experimenters and first-line managers in regional governance…. The key to American competitiveness is, as it always has been, a dynamic, innovative, market-driven private sector. The responsibility for achieving it belongs principally to the private sector itself. But the private sector will be successful only through partnership with government at all levels. Some states are well advanced in holding up their end of the bargain. — R.Scott Fosler, *The New Economic Role of American States*[1]

As Fosler observed, state economic development programs have changed substantially during the past two decades. The objective of this chapter is to provide a broader setting for understanding the nature of recent innovative programs and the context for evaluating various strategies to improve rural competitiveness, which are discussed in chapter 4. An important theme, addressed at the end of this chapter, is the equity concern raised in chapter 2: To what extent are the benefits from state economic development programs flowing to rural communities? How well do existing economic development programs meet the needs of rural economies? Should special initiatives be developed to assist rural communities?

For more than half a century, the primary focus of state and local economic development efforts has been to lure new businesses to their jurisdictions from somewhere else. These efforts have been called recruitment or "smokestack chasing." The primary enticement to a firm to locate in a specific jurisdiction has been the offer of special tax abatements and generous loan programs. Many rural communities, especially in the South, have used this general strategy.

Beginning in the slower growth decade of the 1970s, more jurisdictions sought to compete in this bidding war for new businesses and, consequently, the enticements became more attractive. Two complementary forces were significant: first, the so-called "frost-belt states" were experiencing economic stagnation during much of the 1970s while the "sun-belt states" were growing at a faster rate than the rest of the nation. The stark differences in regional growth patterns led many of the frost-belt states to develop and aggressively market competitive recruitment programs. Second, beginning in the 1970s many of the larger cities felt threatened by the exodus of urban jobs; they also developed economic development programs that used tax subsidies and financial packages both to recruit and to retain existing firms.

The prominent visibility of these programs provoked criticism of the basic strategy of bidding for business. Critics and taxpayers began to question whether the cost of enticements was justified. Other questions were asked: Who would get these new jobs from the recruited firm? What is the public cost per job created? What kind of multiplier effects — the number of secondary jobs created — could be anticipated? Would the recruited firm stay after the tax subsidy expired or would it flee to the best deal available in another jurisdiction? Would the generous subsidy increase the burden on existing taxpayers or lead to public service reductions? What is the actual public benefit from the recruited firm?[2] In addition to these questions, existing businesses have often expressed the concern that their needs were being neglected by the dominant strategy of recruiting new firms.

In 1992, Illinois Governor Jim Edgar, as chair of the National Governors' Association Committee on Economic Development and Technological Innovation, sought to deescalate the bidding war for business by job-hungry states. Yet, later that year, a *Business Week* article noted that during 1992 "Indiana lured a United Airlines maintenance facility with a $1 billion package, South Carolina gave BMW $130 million for an assembly plant, and Minnesota provided $835 million to snare maintenance shops for Northwest Airlines."[3] According to his staff, Governor Edgar has said, "A lot of governors want to disarm, but they don't want to disarm unilaterally."[4]

The governor's press secretary, John Truscott, observed that "States are getting in the precarious position of buying jobs. That puts existing local businesses in the position of funding their competition."[5] In addition, the perception of negotiating a lucrative deal has caused voter backlash: "The mayor of Flat Rock, Michigan, was voted out largely because of anger about the 14-year tax holiday given to Mazda Motor Corporation."[6] (See box 3-1 for an academic overview of industrial incentives.)

Despite these controversies, the recruitment of new firms has continued to be an important activity of most state economic development agencies because it serves important political and institutional needs. Elected officials derive positive public relations benefits from the ribbon-cutting attention given by the media to successful recruitment activities. Enticing a new firm to locate within a jurisdiction is an important symbol for elected officials of their commitment to creating more employment and the uncritical media attention is highly valued by politicians. Hence, economic development officials are successful in their jobs (as well as protecting their budgets and enhancing their own careers) when they succeed in negotiating these deals. Luring a new firm to a jurisdiction has been referred to as "shooting a buffalo" by professional recruiters. It is difficult to reform a process that generates institutional benefits to elected officials, career professionals, and the media.

The emerging scrutiny of location incentives has resulted in more sophisticated legal contracts to establish performance standards for the resulting employment and taxes generated from these deals. "Clawbacks" has become the general phrase for those legal provisions to reclaim or recalibrate "all or some of a financing package when a firm fails to meet performance requirements." Clawbacks have been common in Europe, but only in recent years have they been used by state and local governments.[7] One prominent example occurred when Governor Evan Bayh of Indiana wrote strong clawbacks into the United deal. According to a *Business Week* article:

> Bayh set up the deal so that the state would get its money back in payroll taxes and other ripple effects within 15 years…. The airline guaranteed that it will spend $800 million on the maintenance facility by the year 2002 and employ 6,300 people there by the year 2005 (emphasis added).[8]

Although recruitment and retention efforts often rank high on state and local economic development agendas, other strategies have been advanced by the states during the 1980s. One of the key findings of a 1986 study by the National Governors' Association was that "The smokestack-chasing of the sixties is being complemented by more sophisticated development tools and techniques. While industrial recruitment activities continue, *new economic development efforts are geared to enhancing existing state businesses, developing new indigenous companies and products, and expanding into international markets*" (original emphasis).[9]

Most of the innovative state economic development programs developed in the 1980s had these four objectives: to assist small businesses, to modernize manufacturing, to pursue high-technology development, and to gain foreign markets or investment. Each of these four strategies is briefly summarized below:

Small Business Development: Empirical support for this strategy came from David Birch's research that small businesses — those with fewer than twenty employees — produced 80 percent of the net increase in employment between 1969 and 1976. (For more about the study, see "Promoting Entrepreneurship" in chapter 4.)[10] A 1989 study by the National Governors' Association (NGA) entitled *Promoting Technological Excellence: the Role of State and Federal Extension Activities* identified through a national survey more than 200 programs providing direct assistance to small business; these services included "help preparing a business plan or

Box 3-1
Industrial Incentives: An Academic Overview

I am not going to tell you that incentives do not work. Our whole economic system is based on competition and incentives. However, there is nothing in the literature that says they invariably work, from the macro picture. Also, there is no evidence that they work over time. In fact, there is considerable evidence that if everyone gives them and they are basically the same, you are in a zero-sum game.

There are exceptions. In a global competitive world where all states are not the same and all incentives are not the same, some incentives are probably better than others. Specific incentives under specific circumstances can work. Unfortunately, we do not know which ones under which circumstances are going to be the best and how to measure their benefits over time.

There is agreement among everyone that (incentives) are less effective because the economy has changed. Quality is more important than cost. Stability is more important than an incentive. There is also agreement that incentives will provide few net new jobs to the economy. One can expect a decline in the use of incentives both by the giver and the taker. (Businesses) are looking at the things that states do that affect the economy from provid-

identifying sources of financing as well as those that emphasize technology assistance, specialized services such as product testing, or help with engineering problems." [11]

Modernization of Manufacturing: Another study by NGA (1991), identified forty-two programs in twenty-eight states, of which more than 84 percent were established since 1980, that provided technological assistance to small and medium-sized manufacturers; "Total funding for fiscal 1991 was $83 million. Slightly more than 45 percent of this funding came directly from state government. Another 11 percent came from state universities." [12]

High Technology Development: By the mid-1980s, "34 states were pursuing high technology development through science parks and development corporations, 40 were offering programs of technical assistance, and

---

ing education to building roads. *There is little that Governors do that does not affect the economy. Incentives are just a small piece of that.*

The political risks (from using incentives) are on the rise. The media has examples of incentives that have fallen apart. It is no longer a win/win situation. In fact, there is a wonderful opportunity for Governors to take credit for defusing these border incentive wars. There is also an opportunity for the National Governors' Association to work with business to say that "it takes two to tango." It is not just interjurisdictional competition that feeds the incentive frenzy. If incentives actually mean less to the business decision, it would be useful for responsible business groups to say so.

The shadow on the horizon is the fact that the incentives race is spreading to other regions of the world. It is now a global competition.

Source: Excerpts from Professor Don Haider's presentation at the NGA Economic Development and Technological Innovation Committee meeting on February 2, 1992; as quoted in Jay Kayne, *Investing America's Economic Future: States and Industrial Incentives* (National Governors' Association, 1992), 5, (original emphasis).

44 were operating university-based centers for technology development."[13] A 1987 survey by the Minnesota Department of Trade and Economic Development reported that 43 states had at least one program encouraging technological innovation, and that more than $550 million were being spent by states during FY 1988 for science and technology initiatives.[14] According to Walter Plosila, an economic development official in Maryland, about half of the states offer aid directly to inventors at universities; Utah's Centers of Excellence program, which directs state funds to inventors to produce cutting-edge commercial projects, is among "the nation's most innovative projects in creating jobs."[15] However, a 1991 study concluded that "Many states with more enlightened programs do not have an explicit rural focus to their high-tech efforts. Therefore, the most rural communities can expect is that benefits of high-tech policy will trickle down over time...."[16]

International Activities: State economic development programs, according to the National Association of State Development Agencies, spent more than $90 million annually on international activities by 1990, which included both export assistance and foreign investment recruitment.[17]

In *The Rise of the Entrepreneurial State: State and Local Economic Development Policy in the United States*, Peter Eisenger referred to these innovative programs as "demand-side" stimulation for state economies in contrast to such "supply-side" inducements as low business taxes, industrial revenue bonds, and tax abatements. Eisenger argued that:

> Investment, which in turn generates jobs, would be attracted to those locales where the costs of factors of production...are lower. Thus, northern states have set out to match their competition by offering the same or even more generous location inducements to mobile firms. But the putative value of these inducements, whose efficacy economists have doubted from the beginning, have diminished as more and more states have offered them, creating incentives to experiment with new policies that promoted development in noncompetitive ways. The result has been the profusion of policies identified with the entrepreneurial state, which *emphasize local resources as the basis for growth rather than the competitive engagement of other states for mobile capital* (emphasis added).[18]

Most researchers of state economic development programs have concluded that traditional financial inducement programs spend more public dollars than the newer programs that aid small businesses and new ventures. Timothy Bartik in his book, *Who Benefits from State and Local Economic Development Policies?*, noted that state development agencies spent about $1.5 billion in 1990 and that state spending on high technology was estimated at $550 million in 1988. He concluded "Even if there were no overlap, and all of this $2 billion was devoted to new wave programs, these expenditures are dwarfed by the various tax subsidies, or "tax expenditures," that state and local governments give to business for economic development purposes." [19] (Box 3-2 presents Bartik's "A Typology of State and Local Economic Development Policies that Directly Aid Businesses.")

During the 1980s, economic development practitioners argued about which approach—supply side or the newer programs to foster homegrown businesses — was more effective. In 1990, Doug Ross and Robert Friedman critiqued both in their article "The Emerging Third Wave: New Economic Development Strategies." [20]

According to the authors, recruitment efforts, or in their words "Chasing the almighty smokestack," were part of the "first wave" of development policies. They explained that:

> The reason First Wave development policies worked from the '50s to the '70s, especially in the poor states, was because at that point corporations were seeking the cheapest locations for branch plant operations that relied primarily on the use of unskilled labor. Moreover, most firms limited their searches to the continental United States.[21]

They argued that this approach changed as the most competitive corporations went global in search of even lower costs of production:

> Companies looking for cheap, unskilled labor and low-cost locations were no longer confined to the U.S. As inexpensive as rural Mississippi or some Sunbelt locale might be, Mexico was cheaper, and Sri Lanka cheaper yet. No matter how large their incentives or low their wages or taxes, U.S. communities could no longer compete as the lowest-cost location for production.

They also noted that the global competition for higher quality goods appeared to result from the increasing sophistication of technology in manufacturing production and that "generated a growing demand for more educated workers and higher technology capabilities. These resources were not central to most First Wave strategies." [22]

Box 3-2

A Typology of State and Local Economic Development Policies that Directly Aid Businesses

TRADITIONAL ECONOMIC DEVELOPMENT POLICIES
(Primarily Targeted at Branch Plant Recruitment)

Marketing Area as Branch Plant Location
> Industrial development advertising
> Marketing trips to corporate headquarters
> Provision of site information to prospects

Financial Incentives
> Industrial revenue bonds
> Property tax abatements
> Other tax relief
> Provision of land at below-market prices
> Direct state loans

Nonfinancial Incentives to Branch Plants
> Customized industrial training
> Expedited provision of site-specific infrastructure
> Help with regulatory problems

Source: Timothy J. Bartik, *Who Benefits from State and Local Economic Development Policies?* (Kalamazoo, Mich.: W.E. Upjohn Institute for Employment Research, 1991), 4.

According to Ross and Friedman, a "second wave" of development policies began in the 1980s with a focus on "homegrown" or indigenous economic development activity:

> States began to realize that to help their existing firms and attract new investment, the production inputs in the local economy — a skilled workforce, risk capital, available technology, sophisticated management information and modern telecommunications — would have to be world-competitive in quality and cost.

**"NEW WAVE" ECONOMIC DEVELOPMENT POLICIES
(Primarily Targeted at Small or Existing Businesses)**

Capital Market Programs

Predominantly government-financed loan or equity programs
Government support for predominantly privately financed loan or
equity programs

Information/Education for Small Business

Small business ombudsman/information office
Community college classes in starting a business
Small business development centers
Entrepreneurial training programs
Small business incubators

Research and High Technology

Centers of excellence in business-related research at public universities
Research-oriented industrial parks
Applied research grants
Technology transfer programs/industrial extension services

Export Assistance

Information/training in how to export
Trade missions
Export financing

Yet "second wave" programs also had their drawbacks, according to the authors: they lack scale and accountability, service is fragmented, and they seldom link economic and social concerns.[23]

The authors proclaimed that a "third wave" in economic development policies was emerging, which would employ "new organizational approaches to make Second Wave policies truly effective." The most radical, and certainly most sensible, of their proposed third wave principles is the concept that real demand for economic development services must be demonstrated; indeed, "The intended beneficiaries must invest some of their own time or resources in order to obtain the desired service." Other principles were that public resources should seek to leverage private funds; that competition among service providers be encouraged; and that automatic feedback mechanisms are established.[24]

States have experimented with different delivery systems for economic development programs and some of the recent ones have reflected the third wave principles. For example, Oregon has pioneered several new initiatives (such as sectoral networks, which are described in chapter 4) that reflect these third wave principles.[25] Moreover, these principles have also served a very important function in guiding a much broader discussion about "reinventing government."[26]

The third wave principles for organizational design, the emergence of public-private partnerships, and the broader discussion about reinventing government have provoked important debates about accountability, governmental responsibility, and public purpose. Economic development programs "steered" by private sector leaders may be responsive, accountable, and effective in meeting the public's objectives. Occasionally, though, they may not meet these standards. *The responsibility for spending public funds to achieve social purposes should not be casually handed over to public-private partnerships without establishing quantifiable objectives and tough performance standards.*[27]

Economic Development Objectives

Timothy Bartik has concluded that job creation is the primary goal of economic development policies "from the perspective of politicians and voters." He has maintained that economic development policies "will face political death if they fail to increase job growth." [28] Others, though, have suggested that it is the short-term electoral cycle that exerts extreme pressure on the use of job creation as the benchmark for the success of various economic development programs. According to Roger Vaughan, Robert Pollard, and Barbara Dyer in their book, *The Wealth of States: Policies for a Dynamic Economy*, "The pressure on elected officials to do something immediately leads to policies that have (or appear to have) quick and readily observable results, sometimes without regard for their long-term consequences." As an example of this, they observed that, "By subsidizing a firm to move into a state, taxes paid by other firms are driven up, impairing their competitive position." [29]

Perhaps a wasteful, poorly designed public works program serves as a better example of how the immediate pressure for job creation could actually retard rather than advance economic development objectives. Although often touted as part of an economic development program that generates some immediate employment (and modest short-term stimulus), a cluster of "pork barrel" projects could actually produce relatively little of social value and would add much to the tax burden of both firms and workers. In contrast, however, strategic and well-managed public infrastructure investments, such as those in transportation or telecommunication systems, can generate both short-term jobs in construction and contribute to the general economic efficiency of the locality, state, or nation. Similarly, state technology programs that assist firms in developing state-of-the-art applications could, theoretically, both facilitate growth and improve the firms' capability to adapt in the future, although the applications themselves may not increase employment immediately.

Even some of those comfortable with a short-term focus on job creation have asked tough questions: Jobs for whom? Who gets the jobs created from these economic development programs? Are they "good" jobs? Do they pay enough to support an average family? Will they provide sufficient challenges to young people so that they are not tempted to move away from their family, friends, and communities to pursue careers elsewhere? Are they secure jobs? Will they relocate to other jurisdictions later on?

On the broadest level, what is the public benefit from economic development programs? Who benefits directly? Who benefits indirectly? Can these public benefits be measured?

Others are also explicit in emphasizing the difference, as public policy goals, between economic growth and the equitable distribution of the expanded resources. For example, notice how the equity objective is emphasized in this definition:

> Economic development is an increase in economic activity (more or better jobs, housing, or public services) that results in a wider distribution of the quantities being measured (income is more evenly distributed, the housing stock is not simply in a few very large houses) and an economy that is capable of sustaining the higher level of activity in the future from its own resources.[30]

In some cases, the dichotomy between growth and equity is a false one; nevertheless, both of these goals represent social value choices that should theoretically be resolved through the political system: for example, how important is the goal of distributional equity? Is it more important than economic growth and the development of adaptive capacity for the future? As important? Almost as important? These fundamental questions are not often either addressed or resolved through the political process; even when raised explicitly, the states are likely to resolve them differently.

Stripped of the equity objective, the above definition suggests that *economic development is the process of facilitating economic growth and the development of an adaptive capacity to sustain a "higher level of activity in the future from its own resources."* [31] (Box 3-3, excerpted from the *Wealth of the States*, further defines development.) In this era of national restructuring and global competition, it may be helpful for state policymakers to think about what kind of future they are seeking to achieve, and then evaluate how well existing economic development programs either facilitate growth or develop adaptive capacity to sustain future growth. Economist Albert Shapero has articulated this vision by emphasizing essential characteristics of healthy economies:

Box 3-3
What is Economic Development?

First, the goal of economic development is to create wealth. Wealth is our capacity to produce those goods and services that we value, and includes not only those items whose value is established in the market place but also nonmarket goods and services such as a clean environment, justice, and public safety. While job creation is the result of successful policy, it is not in and of itself the goal of economic development. For example, by subsidizing a firm to move into a state, taxes paid by other firms are driven up, impairing their competitive position.

Second, we expand our capacity to produce when risk-taking individuals and public agencies discover and develop better ways to use resources. Public sector activities play a vital role in establishing the climate for entrepreneurial activity by establishing and enforcing rules and regulations and by making needed investments in education and infrastructure.

Third, many traditional development policies — such as industrial recruiting and public works programs — have limited capacity either to spur development or to create jobs. On the other hand, many govern-

What we really want for an area (or more precisely, for the people of an area) is to achieve a state denoted by resilience — the ability to respond to changes in the environment efficiently; creativity and innovativeness — the ability and willingness to experiment and (be) innovative; and initiative taking — the ability, desire, and power to begin and carry through useful projects. Preceding and accompanying the dynamic characteristics of resiliency, creativity and innovativeness, and initiative taking is diversity...(providing) some measure of invulnerability to the effects of many unforeseen events and decisions.[32]

Many economic development objectives are complementary; others conflict. Programs that generate immediate job creation — such as those that

---

ment activities not traditionally regarded as development strategies — such as investments in education and infrastructure and regulatory reform — have a much greater if unexploited potential.

Finally, development policy is conducted in perennial conflict. As purchasers of goods and services, we all benefit from greater choice and lower costs resulting from innovations. But as employees, resource owners, and stockholders we may lose in the development process. To the worker who loses a job because of a new labor saving technology or an increase in imports from abroad, the availability of new products will seem poor compensation. To the investor whose investment fails because the company could not compete, progress brings little reward. The displaced worker and the disappointed investor are part of a constituency that may oppose development. A successful development strategy must include not only the right policies but also ways of resolving or reducing the economic and political conflicts inherent in the policy making process.

Source: Roger Vaughan, Robert Pollard, and Barbara Dyer, *The Wealth of States: Policies for a Dynamic Economy,* (Washington, D.C.: Council of State Planning Agencies, 1985), 1-2, (original emphasis).

entice firms into the state by granting generous subsidies or those inefficient, wasteful public works programs — may stimulate short-term growth, but ultimately diminish the state's adaptive capacity for future, sustainable growth. Both conditions must be met: the first is essential for political and social reasons, and the latter (adaptive capacity) is necessary to sustain growth during an era of rapid change and accelerating global competition.

Economic Development and Rural Competitiveness

How well do existing economic development programs promote rural competitiveness? Traditional economic development programs premised on bidding for mobile businesses by lowering the production costs have been used extensively by rural communities, especially in the South, to lure branch plants to their jurisdictions. Faced with competition from lower-wage, industrializing nations, these financial enticements are not likely to be as effective in the future. Similarly business retention programs may produce short-term benefits for many states and jurisdictions, but would appear to offer meager hope for strengthening the adaptive capacity of state and local economies.

The business assistance programs that have been developed in the past twenty years may enhance the adaptive capacity of state economies. But the scale of these "second wave" programs poses important questions for rural areas. Are these programs adequately serving rural communities? Are the business development centers located in just the larger cities? Are there new and unexplored ways to use advanced technologies such as telecommunication and interactive video systems to conquer geographic space to provide business services in rural communities? In short, are the economic needs of rural communities being addressed by these state programs?

State policymakers confronting the challenge of rural competitiveness should face other questions as well: Are the managers of conventional economic development programs aware of the special needs of rural economies? How much effort is now exerted by state government through its economic development programs to assist rural areas? Is there any evidence to suggest that an institutional bias exists within state economic development agencies against assisting rural communities? Do state economic development agencies or their managers have an antirural bias, conscious or otherwise?

Many rural advocates and scholars allege that our society manifests a consistent antirural bias resulting in minimal media coverage, distorted myths of the problems and opportunities in these areas, and decidedly less-than-benign neglect by the federal and state governments.[33] They may allege, therefore, that a subtle bias, institutional or professional, may be present in some state governments that results in a lower priority for rural concerns than for those of other jurisdictions.[34]

On the other hand, a forthcoming paper by Ronald Ferguson and Dewitt John observed that, "Over 20 states have established offices of rural affairs to help rural communities to access resources in multiple agencies. These offices usually provide technical assistance to rural leaders in dealing with government agencies, and they also are advocates within the bureaucracy for rural concerns."[35] In addition, the governors of the fifteen states attending the CGPA State Policy Academies in 1990 and 1992 demonstrated strong commitments to make substantive policy changes to improve rural competitiveness (see chapter 5). Will these and other states, perhaps aided by the formation of State Rural Development Councils, build upon the initial efforts to promote rural competitiveness?

State policymakers should objectively assess existing state economic development programs because the allegation by rural advocates of an institutional or unconscious antirural bias must not be dismissed out of hand. Indeed, this review may well reveal a lack of special initiatives designed to improve rural competitiveness. Some of the traditional programs may have been designed initially as industrial recruitment programs or to promote development in metropolitan areas. Quite simply, those programs may be ineffective or inappropriate in assisting small towns and rural communities.

It is also important to distinguish between inadvertent neglect and the lack of effective political muscle to reshape state policies and programs. State agencies, of course, are accountable to the governor who appoints their managers, the legislature that approves their budgets and grants them statutory authority to execute their programs, and the public — especially the voters — that wants results and hopes for efficiency.

Consider how different mission statements for state economic development agencies would affect their priorities. For example, one mission statement might be intended to maximize business and employment opportunities in the aggregate within the state and, to that end, the most effective programs would receive the most resources regardless of which areas receive the most benefits. With this mission, rural communities would be less likely to receive equal services, effort, or benefits from conventional economic development programs. A quite different outcome would result if the state economic development agency's primary mission were to promote economic growth in all regions of the state. To achieve such a mission, different strategies and programs would be necessary to provide economic development assistance to rural communities because of their special needs and lack of development capability.

As discussed, many rural communities suffer from three distinct economic disadvantages: lack of scale economies owing to low population densities, the distance penalty or isolation, and limited fiscal and development capacities. In many cases, the existing array of state policies and programs is insufficient to address these particular rural needs. State policymakers and rural advocates should work closely with state legislative leadership to chart political strategies for directing more state resources to improve rural competitiveness.

Summary

State economic development programs have evolved from primarily smokestack chasing to a broad range of programs that are designed to assist existing, and to promote new, small businesses. The latest generation of programs may enhance the adaptive capacity of state economies to innovate and succeed in a competitive and uncertain future.[36] Still evolving are newer experiments that incorporate third wave principles, which may address some of the organizational weaknesses of the current programs. This promising picture is clouded by three concluding observations:

- Severe fiscal constraints have forced state governments to reduce funding for existing programs and agencies; budget reductions are often made indiscriminately — in part, because these programs are so difficult to evaluate objectively; hence, tight state budgets may have adversely affected some of the more promising economic development programs; furthermore, continued state budget crises may be an obstacle to developing new programs and initiatives designed to promote rural competitiveness.

- The scale and design of most of the business assistance programs limit their potential social benefits. For example, only a few businesses that appear at the business development centers on a "first-come, first-serve" basis can be helped. Relatively few efforts have been made to achieve greater accountability for these programs by charging prices to the users, but other "third wave" principles may yet shape subsequent state economic development programs.

- State economic development programs vary considerably in the extent to which they provide special, targeted assistance that meets the unique development needs of rural communities. Substantial progress has been made in many states as policymakers attempt to address these special needs and design effective programs to promote rural competitiveness. Many of these recent attempts are described in chapter 4.

Notes:

1. R. Scott Fosler, *The New Economic Role of American States: Strategies in a Competitive World Economy* (New York: Oxford University Press, 1988), 3.

2. For an early critique of smokestack chasing, see, for example, Robert Goodman, *The Last Entrepreneurs: America's Regional Wars for Jobs and Dollars* (New York: Simon and Schuster, 1979); and for a recent summary of the contemporary issues, see Gary Enos, "Incentives Under Scrutiny: Is Government Giving Away the Farm?" *City and State*, October 19-November 1, 1992, p.1; and Joel Brinkley, "New Challenge for States: Making, Not Taking, Jobs," *New York Times*, 25 November 1992, p.1.

3. James B. Treece with Zachary Schiller and David Greising, "States Now Want a Money-back Guarantee," *Business Week*, 21 September 1992, 35.

4. Gary Enos, "Incentives Under Scrutiny"; see also "Are Economic Development Incentives Smart?" ("Point" is by Kentucky Governor Brereton Jones and "Counterpoint" is by Illinois Governor Jim Edgar) in *State Government News* (Lexington, Ky.: Council of State Governments, March 1993): 12-13.

5. Gary Enos, "Incentives under Scrutiny."

6. Larry C. Ledebur and Douglas Woodward, "Adding a Stick to the Carrot: Location Incentives with Clawbacks, Recisions, and Recalibrations," *Economic Development Quarterly* 4 no.3, (August 1990): 237.

7. Ibid., 221; also, according to *Planning* (Chicago: American Planning Association, April 1993), 34: "A Michigan judge ruled in February that the General Motors Corporation could not shut down its Ypsilanti assembly plant because the town had provided the auto maker a total of $13.5 million in tax abatements in 1984 and 1988. Ypsilanti Township sued GM when the company announced last year that the plant was one of 21 to be closed to cut costs. GM plans to appeal."

8. Treece et al., "Money-back Guarantee," 35.

9. Marianne K. Clarke, *Revitalizing State Economies: A Review of State Economic Development Policies and Programs* (Washington, D.C.: National Governors' Association, 1986), p.xi.

10. Birch, David L., *The Job Generation Process* (Cambridge, Mass.: MIT Program on Neighborhood and Regional Change, 1978).

11. Marianne K. Clarke and Eric N. Dobson, *Promoting Technological Excellence: the Role of State and Federal Extension Activities* (Washington, D.C.: National Governors' Association, 1989).

12. Marianne K. Clarke and Eric N. Dobson, *Increasing the Competitiveness of America's Manufacturers: A Review of State Industrial Extension Programs* (Washington, D.C.: National Governors' Association, 1991), p.vii.

13. R. Scott Fosler, "State Economic Policy: The Emerging Paradigm" in *Economic Development Quarterly* 6, no.1 (February 1992): 6. The survey was conducted in 1984 by *High Technology* magazine and is summarized by Peter K. Eisinger in *The Rise of the Entrepreneurial State: State and Local Economic Development Policy in the United States* (Madison: University of Wisconsin Press, 1988), 281.

14. Irwin Feller, "American State Governments as Models for National Science Policy," *Journal of Policy Analysis and Management* 11, no. 2 (Spring 1992): 290.

15. Joel Brinkley, "New Challenge for States: Making, Not Taking, Jobs," *New York Times*, 25 November 1992.

16. Amy K. Glasmeier, *The High-Tech Potential: Economic Development in Rural America* (New Brunswick, N.J.: Center for Urban Policy Research/Rutgers University, 1991), 188.

17. William E. Nothdurft, *Going Global: How Europe Helps Small Firms Export* (Washington, D.C.: Brookings, 1992), 90.

18. Peter K. Eisenger, *The Rise of the Entrepreneurial State* (Madison: University of Wisconsin Press, 1988) 10-11. A note of clarification on the terminology: some of what Eisenger refers to as demand-side is a nonfinancial form of supply-side assistance. Technical assistance and services to small businesses are two examples of programs that reduce supply-side costs of production in much the same way that loan subsidies or tax abatements reduce the supply-side production costs. Using the economists' terminology, an example of demand-side assistance would be a state procurement program that gave preference to goods and services provided by in-state businesses.

19. Timothy J. Bartik, *Who Benefits From State and Local Economic Development Policies?* (Kalamazoo, Mich.: W.E.Upjohn Institute, 1991), 6.

20. Doug Ross and Robert E. Friedman, "The Emerging Third Wave: New Economic Development Strategies," *Local Economic Development: Strategies for a Changing Economy*, R. Scott Fosler, ed.,(Washington, D.C.: International City Management Association, 1991): 125-137; The article first appeared in the *Entrepreneurial Economy Review* (Autumn 1990) published by the Corporation For Enterprise Development.

21. Ross and Friedman, "Emerging Third Wave," 126.

22. Ibid., 127. These authors could well have quoted David Hume who wrote in the eighteenth century: "Manufactures...gradually shift their places, leaving those countries and provinces which they have already enriched, and flying to others, whither they are allured by the cheapness of provisions and labour; till they have enriched there also, and are again banished by the same causes." E. Rotwein (ed.) *David Hume, Writings on Economics* (Madison: University of Wisconsin Press, 1955), 34-35 as quoted in Rostow, W.W. *Theorists of Economic Growth from David Hume to the Present* (New York: Oxford University Press, 1990), 30.

23. Ross and Friedman, "Emerging Third Wave," 130-131.

24. Ibid., 132-134; One of the better summaries of the Third Wave concept is in Timothy J. Bartik, "Federal Policy Towards State and Local Economic Development in the 1990s," working paper, W. E. Upjohn Institute for Employment Research, Kalamazoo, Michigan, March 1993. Here are two excerpts:

> In the last few years, some activists have promoted a new approach to economic development labelled the Third Wave. The Third Wave concept is that rather than having government directly provide economic development services to small and existing businesses, the government should encourage private sector providers, ideally operating in a competitive market, to provide such economic development services. Under the Third Wave approach, the government would still be involved with economic development, because it would pro-

vide some subsidies and guidance to these private or quasi-private economic development service providers. But government would only pay a portion rather than 100% of the cost of providing economic development services. [P.5]

The Third Wave has arisen in response to disappointment over the political and practical feasibility of Second Wave programs in which governments directly provide services to small and existing businesses. Second Wave programs suffer from four interrelated problems: insufficient size to have significant effects, fragmented services, lack of accountability, and lack of business support. It is politically difficult to ever expand Second Wave programs, in which governments pay 100% of the costs of providing services to selected businesses, to a sufficient size to significantly affect a state or metropolitan area's economic growth. Services provided are fragmented. One government office helping with exporting, another with modernization, and a third with job training. As with most government services, objective evaluations of the performance of Second Wave programs are rare. No market test prevents a bad program from continuing. Business support for Second Wave programs is weak. Most businesses have no interest in going to some government agency for advice. Without business support, Second Wave programs are vulnerable to changes in political fashion and budgetary problems in state and local governments.

The Third Wave approach in theory solves these problems. By working through private or quasi-private organizations, Third Wave programs are supposed to be able to provide more flexible and better integrated services to businesses. Private and quasi-private organizations also are supposed to elicit more business support. Because the government subsidy for services is considerably less than 100%, a given government budget for economic development can potentially provide services to more firms. Furthermore, because part of the costs of economic development services are borne by business clients, there is at least some minimum accountability. Businesses will not pay fees for services unless they feel they are of some value. [Pp. 7-8]

25. Joseph Cortright, "Third Wave Economic Development in Oregon" (Oregon Joint Legislative Committee on Trade and Economic Development, Salem, Oregon, December 1991).

26. See David Osborne and Ted Gaebler, *Reinventing Government: How the Entrepreneurial Spirit is Transforming the Public Sector* (New York: Addison-Wesley, 1992); and, especially, Michael Barzeley with Barak Armajani, *Breaking Through Bureaucracy: A New Vision for Managing in Government* (Berkeley: University of California Press, 1992).

27. See Donald F. Kettl, *Sharing Power: Public Governance and Private Markets* (Washington, D.C.: The Brookings Institution, 1993); also see note number 7, chapter 5.

28. Bartik, *Who Benefits*, 6.

29. Roger Vaughan, Robert Pollard, and Barbara Dyer, *The Wealth of States: Policies for a Dynamic Economy* (Washington, D.C.: CSPA, 1985), 2.

30. Julia Ann Parzen and Michael Hall Kieschnick, *Credit Where It's Due: Development Banking for Communities* (Philadelphia, Pa.: Temple University Press, 1992), 4.

31. For those seeking a more formal discussion of the concept of development, note this excerpt from Joseph A. Schumpeter's *The Theory of Economic Development* (Cambridge: Harvard University Press, 1955), 63-4 and 66; as quoted in W.W.Rostow, Theorists of Economic Growth from David Hume to the Present (New York: Oxford University Press, 1990), 235:

Development in our sense is a distinct phenomenon, entirely foreign to what may be observed in the circular flow or in the tendency toward equilibrium. It is spontaneous and discontinuous change in the channels of the flow, disturbance of equilibrium, which forever alters and displaces the equilibrium state previously existing....

This concept covers the following five cases: (1) the introduction of a new good—that is one with which the consumers are not yet familiar—or of a new quality of good. (2) The introduction of a new method of production, that is one not yet tested by experience in the branch of manufacture concerned, which need by no means be founded upon a discovery scientifically new, and can also exist in a new way of handling a commodity commercially. (3) The opening of a new market, that is a market into which the particular branch of manufacture of the country in question has not previously entered, whether or not this market has existed before. (4) The conquest of a new source of supply of raw materials of half-manufactured goods, again irrespective of whether this source already exists or whether it has first to be created. (5) The carrying out of the new organization of any industry, like the creation of a monopoly position...or the breaking up of a monopoly position.

32. Albert Shapero, "The Role of Entrepreneurship in Economic Development at the Less-Than-National Level" in *Expanding the Opportunity to Produce: Revitalizing the American Economy Through New Enterprise Development*, ed., Robert Friedman and William Schweke, (Washington, D.C.: Corporation for Enterprise Development, 1981), 26-27, as quoted in William E. Nothdurft, *Renewing America: Natural Resource Assets and State Economic Development* (Washington, D.C.: Council of State Planning Agencies, 1984), 167.

33. Some of the contributors in the book, *Rural Policies for the 1990s*, ed., Cornelia B. Flora and James A. Christenson (Boulder, Colo.: Westview Press, 1991) make these allegations.

34. A majority of the state economic development program managers live and work in urban areas. Most of their professional experience is likely to have come from working in metropolitan areas on economic development projects common to urban and suburban environments for the simple reason that those jurisdictions have the resources to hire professionals. Many of them have received their professional educations in urban planning programs. It would be highly unfair to suggest that these managers, simply because of their personal backgrounds and long years of professional experience, have profound or even subtle biases against rural communities. Such an implication is not intended here. The point simply is that not unlike everyone else economic development managers might prefer to work on those programs and in those jurisdictions with which they are most familiar and comfortable. In short, how well do the managers of state economic development programs understand the special needs of rural communities? Are the state programs they manage responsive to these needs?

35. Ronald F. Ferguson and Dewitt John, *Developing Rural America for 21st Century Competitiveness: The Emerging Movement and the Critical Ideas Behind Best Practices,* Working Draft (Washington, D.C.: Aspen Institute, forthcoming), 80.

36. A State and Local Economic Development Strategy Summit held in December 1992 by the Hubert H. Humphrey Institute of Public Affairs at the University of Minnesota and cosponsored by the National Conference of State Legislatures and the Freeman Center for International Economic Policy also at the Humphrey Institute produced the following summary of future policy directions:

State governments should have explicit economic development strategies with measurable benchmarks to evaluate success and define areas for improvement.

Economic development strategies should focus on enhancing productivity and the comparative advantages of a state or community rather than "zero-sum" game bidding strategies to attract businesses from other areas.

Evaluation should be an integral part of state and local economic development strategies and should experiment with new approaches.

The measures of success for an economic development strategy should be its contribution to increasing productivity and increasing economic participation by all sectors of society.

The federal government should provide the overall vision for the nation's economy and work in partnership with state and local governments to achieve this vision.

See *State and Local Economic Development Strategy Summit: Summary of Presentations and Discussions*, December 3-5, 1992, summarized by Susan Koch, Hubert H. Humphrey Institute of Public Affairs, University of Minnesota, December 1992.

Also see *The 1992 Development Report Card for the States: Economic Benchmarks for State and Corporate Decisionmakers*, sixth edition, (Washington, D.C.: Corporation for Enterprise Development, 1992).

CHAPTER 4

Strategies for Rural Competitiveness

After some four decades of concerted attention to the challenge of development, we might ask how much economics can explain. Economic theory can determine the necessary, though not the sufficient, conditions of growth. The so-called noneconomic factors account for the gap between the necessary and sufficient.... — Paul N. Rosenstein-Rodan[1]

Economic growth depends on attitudes to work, to wealth, to thrift, to having children, to invention, to strangers, to adventure, and so on, and all these attitudes flow from deep springs in the human mind. There have been attempts to explain why these attitudes vary from one community to another. One can look to differences in religion, but this is merely to restate the problem.... The experienced sociologist knows that these questions are unanswerable, certainly in our present state of knowledge, and probably for all time.... What follows is that we should be modest in our claims, and recognize how tentative is any hypothesis which we claim to base upon the study of history. — Arthur Lewis[2]

These are significant concessions by economists — there is much we do not know about economic growth and development. To use Rosenstein-Rodan's phrase, we have learned a great deal about what is necessary for economic growth, but we are still trying to discover the sufficient conditions for growth. The classical economists identified three factors that determined economic growth — capital, labor, and land. The globally competitive economy is a good deal more complicated than that classic formula. The contribution of land (including natural resources) to national wealth has diminished, but land has been rural America's historic comparative advantage. According to Peter Drucker, it has been "uncoupled" as a central factor in the growth equation.[3] To remain viable in the future, rural economies will need to invest strategically now to achieve greater diversity, to prepare workers for different jobs, to develop advanced telecommunications systems, and to create direct linkages (such as networks) with urban, national, and international markets.

This chapter summarizes state government strategies to promote rural competitiveness. It relies heavily upon the experiences of state policymakers and economic development practitioners who have experimented with different organizational approaches, innovative delivery systems, and creative strategies to make rural communities economically competitive. Different strategies work in different circumstances. Diverse rural communities have different needs and will require specialized programs. Some of these programs may neatly fit within the policy and political environment of another state; others will have to be refined and adapted according to special circumstances. To enhance the utility of this material to state policymakers, short resources sections follow the narrative on each of the following rural competitiveness strategies:

• Human Capital (education and training);

• Telecommunications and Advanced Technologies;

• Promoting Entrepreneurship;

• Access to Capital;

• Natural Resources Development;

• Collaborative Efforts on Rural Development;

• Community Leadership and Capacity Building; and

• Public Infrastructure.

Human Capital

The term "human capital" was coined by Nobel Laureate economist Theodore Schultz in his 1961 book, *Investing in Ourselves*, in which he "argued that investments in education and skills were as important, if not more important, than investments in physical capital for less-developed countries."[4] Management expert Peter Drucker made the same assessment:

A little reflection will show that the rate of capital formation to which economists give so much attention is a secondary factor.... The basic factor in an economy's development must be the rate at which a country produces people with imagination and vision, education, theoretical and analytical skills.[5]

In 1990 the National Center on Education and the Economy published a report with an ominous title: *America's Choice: high skills or low wages!*. The report argued persuasively that the numerous deficiencies in the nation's education and training systems, *especially compared with those of our strongest economic competitors*, were undermining our prospects for future prosperity. The report's recommendations included establishing new educational performance standards for all students; developing a system of technical and professional training opportunities for non-college-bound youth; and encouraging employers to invest in additional education and training opportunities for their workers.[6] (Box 4-1 presents an excerpt from the executive summary of this report.) Not so long ago a similar analysis was offered by the *Wall Street Journal:*

Jobs are becoming more demanding, more complex. But our schools don't seem up to the task. They are producing students who lack the skills that business so desperately needs to compete in today's global economy. And in doing so, they are condemning students to a life devoid of meaningful employment.[7]

In *America and the New Economy*, a study of national economic restructuring, Anthony Carnevale noted that:

Despite flat overall wage growth, there have been dramatic shifts in earnings among different groups of Americans. Wage increases in the new economy are rationed with an increasingly uneven hand, resulting in a growing maldistribution of income in the United States. More now than ever, *learning is the rationing hand that distributes earnings in the American economy. People with the most education and access to learning on the job are doing best; those with the least education and least access to learning on the job are doing worst.* (Emphasis added.) [8]

Norman Reid has provided two additional reasons that education and worker skill levels became more important to the improved economic competitiveness of rural communities during the 1980s. He wrote:

Both nationally and in rural areas, job growth has been strongest in industries and occupations demanding high levels of education and skills. Education also appears to be important to the development of new businesses. Research indicates that the people who are most likely to start new rural businesses are those who already live in these areas. That startup rates are highest in areas with higher average levels of education underscores the importance of skills and training to locally generated development as well.[9]

Box 4-1
America's Choice: High Skills or Low Wages, Executive Summary

ANOTHER WAY

While the foreign nations we studied differ in economy and culture, they share an approach to the education and training of their workers and to high productivity work organization.

- They insist that virtually all of their students reach a high educational standard. We do not.

- They provide 'professionalized' education to non-college-bound students to prepare them for their trades and to ease their school-to-work transition. We do not.

- They operate comprehensive labor market systems which combine training, labor market information, job search, and income maintenance for the unemployed. We do not.

- They support company-based training through general revenue or payroll tax based financing schemes. We do not.

- They have national consensus on the importance of moving to high productivity forms of work organization and building high wage economies. We do not.

Our approaches have served us well in the past. They will not serve us well in the future.

Investment in human capital is likely to be the best, long-term economic development strategy for rural America, despite the following observations:

- The concept of investment includes risk and uncertain returns; as is true of other forms of investment, there is no guarantee that the initial expenditures in human capital will yield either immediate or bountiful results. The greatest returns may accrue to communities with the poorest educational systems, or to communities that make other strategic investments, such as telecommunication systems, which complement educational improvement.

THE CHOICE

Americans are unwittingly making a choice. It is a choice that most of us would probably not make were we aware of its consequences. Yet every day, that choice is becoming more difficult to reverse. It is a choice which undermines the American dream of economic opportunity for all. It is a choice that will lead to an America where 30 percent of our people may do well — at least for awhile — but the other 70 percent will see their dreams slip away.

The choice that America faces is a choice between high skills and low wages. Gradually, silently, we are choosing low wages.

We still have time to make the other choice — one that will lead us to a more prosperous future. To make this choice, we must fundamentally change our approach to work and education.

Source: America's Choice: high skills or low wages!, Report of the Commission on the Skills of the American Workforce, (National Center on Education and the Economy, Rochester, N.Y.: June 1990), 4-5.

- Some of the social benefits from improving schools, for example, may be lost to the community that financed them, if local graduates leave and do not return later. In other situations, the confluence of structural forces such as trade and macroeconomic policies may overwhelm the short-term positive benefits from providing quality education. Both of these situations were observed during the troublesome 1980s when many rural communities in the Midwest (for example, Minnesota, Wisconsin, and Michigan) and in the Great Plain States of Nebraska, Iowa, and the Dakotas lost population and local employment even though the quality of local education provided appeared to have been above the national average (as measured by low high school dropout rates and high standardized test scores).

The efficacy of education as an economic development strategy for rural America was questioned in a 1991 report by the Economic Research Service (ERS) entitled, *Education and Rural Economic Development*.[10] One of the chapters in this volume found "a statistically significant association between the average education of nonmetro commuting zones in 1980 and subsequent employment growth in 1980-88," which supported the human capital investment argument. The article, however, found other characteristics that were more important determinants of local growth than local educational levels.[11]

The report observed that educational attainment and worker skill levels were lower in nonmetropolitan counties than in metro counties. Yet, it concluded that "low education levels, at least, were not at the root of the problems facing rural areas in the 1980s." Instead, there appeared to have been a "demand" problem for higher educated rural workers, demonstrated by a "brain-drain" (an exodus of these workers from rural areas) and lower rate of wage increases for these workers in nonmetropolitan counties than those gained by higher educated urban workers during this period. The two phenomenon were mutually reinforcing.[12]

The prospect of rural competitiveness has been diminished by the relocation of higher educated rural workers to urban areas during the 1980s; this movement left rural communities less attractive to those firms seeking better educated employees. Put bluntly, *perpetuating the educational and worker skill deficiencies in rural America, as compared to the metro areas, will severely limit the ability of non-metro areas to adapt to and incorporate new forms of wealth creation.* The information-based economy of the future will require more education and higher skill levels. If rural America lacks the human capital to fulfill these functions, then those jobs — which are mobile — will find educated and skilled workers in other parts of the globe.

The conclusion of the final chapter of this report reflected the traditional economic view on the value of education in fostering economic development:

> Rural areas differ greatly, and new economic trends in technology and trade are likely to affect some local economies more quickly or more extensively than others. If the skill-upgrading challenge is met, however, the rise of the new economy could provide growth opportunities for many rural areas.[13]

The ERS report identified several reasons that educational improvements may be difficult to achieve in rural communities: (1) lower educational aspirations and achievements than urban youth; (2) improvements cost money and many rural areas already face fiscal stress; (3) questions about the efficacy of better schools in terms of "direct payoffs" for the local community; and (4) fewer opportunities for postsecondary education in most rural communities.[14] *These are, however, precisely the kinds of strategies for rural competitiveness that lie within the ability of state policymakers and rural community leaders to shape.* Rural advocates and community leaders should be demanding that educational standards be raised both within their communities and throughout their state.

Above all else, education is a moral responsibility for a society to preserve and protect its culture; in addition, it serves individuals who discover and develop innate abilities and then use them to pursue personal opportunities; and, finally, it provides a collective opportunity to the community to improve its economic viability. The opposition to reforming educational systems and improving training programs has come from several sources: institutional inertia, the resistance of voters, and the opposition of others who doubt the efficacy of investment in human capital as an effective local economic development strategy.

Institutional opposition to raising educational standards and devising new training programs may come from both teachers and parents, from employees and employers, and from other service providers who view reform as a veiled threat to their current mode of operations. Voter opposition is often greatest in rural communities with: (1) large retiree populations that are less willing to finance investment in their youth; (2) trends of population declines and an exodus by young people, who have left to pursue career and social opportunities elsewhere ("Why bother to make the schools any better? They leave after they graduate anyway."); and (3) cultural conservativism about the traditional approaches ("If the school was good enough for me, it is good enough for my kids"). Leadership in behalf of educational improvement in those communities will require a long-term commitment.

State policymakers can focus on the educational financing problems. A forthcoming report by the U.S. Department of Education, *The Condition of Education in Rural Schools*, presents a comprehensive description of the needs of chronically underfunded rural schools. According to this study, rural school districts often have low fiscal capacity from which to raise local funds to support public education; most states do not sufficiently fund their fiscal equalization grant programs to school districts, which places greater local tax burdens on less wealthy jurisdictions; rural school districts often are inadequately compensated under certain categorical programs; and rural school districts may be disadvantaged under current state formulae to fund pupil transportation expenses. Other important issues relating to small, rural schools are discussed in this report as well.[15]

During the past two decades, twenty-six states have witnessed legal challenges to their educational financing systems. The highest courts in ten of these states have ruled that their school finance systems were unconstitutional and have directed their state legislatures to enact systems in which the extent of school financial support is not largely determined by a student's residency. According to this study, "Rural school districts, with their modest fiscal bases, usually cannot generate sufficient local fiscal resources to supplement adequately the state programs in the way that more affluent localities can." The study also quoted from Kern Alexander, an educational finance expert:

> The problems of rural living…are nowhere more obvious than in the underfinanced local school systems that are found in every state in the nation. Rural schools in all states have less money and poorer educational programs than their more wealthy neighbors in urban areas.[16]

A priority objective of state policymakers seeking to improve rural competitiveness should be the reform of educational finance systems that currently disadvantage rural communities by denying educational opportunities to rural students and, simultaneously, placing undue property tax burdens on rural taxpayers. The reform of other delivery systems — such as worker training, health, or social services — to better meet the special needs of rural communities pale in significance to the potential social benefits from achieving meaningful educational finance reform. Indeed, school finance reform often precedes other important school management and improvement objectives. Kentucky's recent overhaul of its state educational system is a case in point:

Educational leaders in the 66 rural districts united to challenge the state's funding formula in 1989...the Kentucky supreme court determined that the entire state system was unconstitutional. The 1990 measure that was the governor's and legislature's response to that landmark decision addressed not only finance, but...curriculum, professional development, at-risk students, and governance.[17]

Despite their weak fiscal capacities and the inequities of state equalization formulae, rural schools have been "in the forefront of developing innovative uses of instructional technology" (that is, telecommunications). Often called distance learning, there are three basic systems that have provided additional course offerings, enrichment material, and instruction to rural students: through a satellite, audiographics, and two-way (interactive) television. More than 20 percent of the school districts with fewer than one thousand students now have a satellite system. This system presents an image of a teacher in multiple receiving site classrooms, which works well for the traditional lecture format. Two-way communication is also often provided through a telephone hookup. Audiographic teleteaching refers "to a small network of compatible personal computers and can be quickly created and disbanded as need dictates...this approach allows considerable control over course content and may be preferred by some districts. But students cannot see the teacher." The two-way television provides totally interactive communication and has been effective with younger and less motivated students, but both equipment and maintenance are expensive.[18]

These technologies provide far more than additional course offerings to rural students. They offer ideas, information, and knowledge that could challenge and stimulate students about the world beyond their own county. One would hope that rural educators will be able to use these technologies to raise educational aspiration levels. It would be unfortunate if other segments of the community such as adult learning, literacy, and General Equivalency Diploma (GED) programs were not also given the opportunity to use these technologies. They could partly mitigate the historic disadvantage of rural isolation and the resulting delay in obtaining new ideas and information.

State governments have responded differently to the challenges of preparing non-college-bound youth for employment and retraining current workers with new skills. Some states do little more than maximize the use of the federal funds available through the Jobs Training Partnership Act. Both topics are very important to those seeking to improve the economic competitiveness of rural areas. They also have in common with education improvement what might be called the supply versus demand problem. In short, why should the public sector invest to improve worker skills if there is no guarantee that the jobs will emerge that require higher skills? Phrased differently, why increase the *supply* of skilled workers when the *demand* for them is either low or uncertain? As with educational improvement, the answer comes in two parts: more highly skilled workers will earn more than those without skills (regardless of location); and those communities with well-educated and trained labor markets will have better and more competitive local economies in the future than those that do not.

Several versions of a new federally funded apprenticeship program modeled after European programs have been proposed in Congress to address the needs of non-college-bound youth and prepare them for the jobs of the future. In addition, a few states have been experimenting with collaborative efforts by vocational education programs, community colleges, and business leaders from the community to provide better job preparation for youth.[19] Better coordination of existing resources, such as the public schools' vocational education programs working closely with the Private Industry Council and local Chambers of Commerce, is especially important for rural communities to focus youth training programs on providing modern skill levels.

The Employment Training Panel in California may be among the most productive and effective state training programs in the country for two reasons — its training programs are designed for experienced workers, not the chronically unemployed and unskilled youth; and the panel uses tough performance standards for the training programs. According to one description of the panel, it "requires that each trainee land a job using his [her] new skills and hold that job at least 90 days. If not, the state takes back all the money it paid to train him [her] — even if the trainee dies…70 percent of the participants fulfill the state's requirements."[20] Other states have gradually increased their own contributions to programs that train experienced workers; to the extent resources allow, these training programs must be stretched to benefit as many rural workers as possible because they are often more vulnerable to sudden job loss than most others in the state.

It is important to repeat, in the language of the economists, that human capital investment is "a necessary, but not sufficient condition for growth." Education and worker training programs are not panaceas; nor can they, by themselves, alone guarantee local or regional economic stability or security.

Resources for Developing a Human Capital Strategy

• American Society for Training and Development, 1640 King Street, Box 1443, Alexandria, Va. 22313; 703.683.8100.

- *America's Choice: high skills or low wages!* National Center on Education and the Economy, 39 State St., Suite 500, Rochester, N.Y. 14614; 716.546.7620.

- *The Condition of Education in Rural Schools*, Office of Educational Research and Improvement, U.S. Department of Education, Room 502J, 555 New Jersey Avenue NW, Washington, D.C. 20208-5644; 202.219.2095, (forthcoming).

- Jobs for the Future, 1815 Massachusetts Avenue, Cambridge, Mass. 02140; 617.661.3411.

Telecommunications and Advanced Technologies

The rapid development of advanced technologies and telecommunication systems represents the greatest potential for stimulating rural economies since the national network of railroads was built over a century ago, which linked much of the continental United States with the rapidly industrializing urban economies (although the Interstate Highway system begun by the federal government in the 1950s was hardly insignificant). A century ago, of course, rural areas were producing food and other raw commodities that fed the urban population and supported its industrialization. In exchange, the rural population received a modest portion of the refined goods and services produced in the cities. Virtually all of the rural economy a century ago was based on natural resources.

The transformation of rural economies during the past century has resulted in somewhat greater diversity and much greater vulnerability to global competition. The employment of all nonmetropolitan counties in 1988 was distributed into these broad categories: 39.8 percent in services; 17.6 percent in manufacturing; 16.8 percent in government; 14.3 percent in other; 9.7 percent in agriculture; and 1.6 percent in mining.[21] Reviewing these aggregates, however, may be misleading because few individual rural counties or regions have this degree of diversity. Many rural areas remain dependent upon a single industry or a handful of large employers.

How successful will rural economies be in competing among global markets? Will the growth sectors of the national economy discover the many comparative advantages offered by rural communities? Will rural communities learn to adapt more effectively and more rapidly to changing economic and social conditions and become more thoroughly integrated into the urban, national, and global economies? What is the role of telecommunication systems in minimizing the distance penalty that has left rural economies lagging behind those of metropolitan areas during the 1980s? Specifically, what should state policymakers do to utilize most efficaciously telecommunication systems as an economic development tool for rural communities?

Telecommunications is a broad term; it means simply the communication of information over distance. Much has changed in the communications industry since dots and dashes were first sent through telegraph wires and Alexander Graham Bell delivered his simple message to his associate Watson. The telephone industry provides voice traffic to virtually every household throughout the nation. The radio and television industries blanket the country with the broadcast of audio and visual materials. The computer industry has developed technologies that enable the rapid movement of data. The development of microwaves, fiber optics, satellite transmission, and other advanced technologies accelerates the movement toward providing interactive, multimedia communications.[22]
The trends in communication technologies are presented in box 4-2.

An excellent report by the congressional Office of Technology Assessment, *Rural America at the Crossroads: Networking for the Future*, provided these basic definitions, although it cautioned that "the boundaries among them are not always clear cut, and are eroding in the face of technological change:"

Box 4-2
Trends in Communication Technologies

- Declining Costs/Increased Performance

- Centralized to Decentralized

- Passive to Interactive

- Single Media to Multimedia

- Increasing Customer Choice

- Disappearing Lines Among Communications Providers

- International Communications Market

Source: Nancy Ginn Helme, *New Alliances in Innovation: A Guide to Encouraging Innovative Applications of New Communication Technologies to Address State Problems.* (Washington, D.C.: Council of Governors' Policy Advisors, 1993), 5.

Information technologies allow individuals to store, process, and reorganize data into a more useful form. Examples include computers, modems, facsimile machines, and answering machines. Access and transmission technologies are the means by which individuals can transmit or receive information from other individuals or information systems. Some examples are cables, radio waves, and satellites. Network technologies are the means by which transmitted information can be managed, routed, and interconnected. These include, for example, switches, bridges, and routers, local area networks (LANS), and signaling systems.[23]

L.C. Mitchell, a telecommunications consultant at Deloitte & Touche who has consulted with New Jersey and Pennsylvania state governments, as quoted in the *N.Y. Times*, observed, "Advanced telecommunications are increasingly being recognized by states as a competitive weapon in economic development and business retention and attraction." [24] Indeed, states have pursued various strategies to promote economic development "including regulatory incentives and reforms; regulatory master planning; deregulation and leadership; public ownership of telecommunication systems; and industry recruitment and development." [25] (See box 4-3.)

Telecommunications represent a tremendous potential to assist rural development, to overcome the economic development disadvantages of isolation and the distance penalty, and to create vital linkages with the robust economic sectors in the urban, national, and global economies. The policy challenge is complicated by numerous factors:

- State legislators and regulators often do not fully comprehend the potential of telecommunications as an economic development tool, especially for rural communities;

- The regulatory transition has changed from pricing subsidies toward pricing at actual costs;

- A broad range of competitors is seeking to meet the new and growing telecommunications demands of urban markets, but often fails to do so in rural communities — effectively outdistancing the technology curve; and

- Many rural communities are already poorly served by the existing services, such as the lack of single-party, touchtone service, which is required to transmit data through computer, modem, and facsimile.

These were among the conclusions presented in *Electronic Byways: State Policies for Rural Development Through Telecommunications*.

The study framed the rural development challenge as follows:

> Rural America faces great risks to its economic well-being if it leaves policy decisions entirely in the hands of the telephone carriers and their regulators, who often are more concerned with the more lucrative and competitive urban markets. Rural leaders must mobilize to prevent rural areas from being hurt in the transition. This period of transition is also a time of genuine opportunity. If rural communities can forge cooperative development plans with development agencies, state government telecommunications network managers, regulatory agencies, and the telecommunications industry, all parties have a unique opportunity to achieve significant benefits.[26]

This study developed broad policy goals and presented specific recommendations to governors and state legislators, development agencies, state regulatory commissions, and telecommunication providers. According to this study, development agencies should:

- Sponsor regional workshops to share information about innovative uses of telecommunications and identify rural telecommunication needs;

- Convene task forces to set goals for modernization of the state's telecommunications infrastructure and plans for its use to stimulate development;

- Build a telecommunications component into small business assistance and rural community development programs;

- Sponsor training courses on telecommunications for community and economic development professionals;

- Work with community colleges to establish telecommunications training courses;

- Encourage the establishment and expansion of distance learning programs for both students and adult education; and

- Work with rural communities and small businesses to help them to obtain collectively the telecommunications services they might not be able to obtain individually.[27]

Edwin B. Parker, a telecommunications consultant and one of the authors of this important book, has emphasized the recommendation that state development agencies should become advocates for rural development interests at the state utility regulatory commission:

I feel that is a particularly important recommendation in these tough budget times, because this is where substantial funds are available for regulatory allocation without new taxes being required. For example, utility commissions have for years supported the policy of universal service — which should help expand rural service. Unfortunately, urban consumer groups, which are very active before regulatory commissions, have made universal service a code word for keeping urban rates low, often at the expense of rural users.

Another example is the persistent use of intra-state long distance rates to subsidize local rates. This is a perverse subsidy that has poorer rural users subsidizing richer urban users, because of the much larger use of intra-state long-distance by rural users. Reducing intra-state long distance rates so that they are closer to the costs of service could provide a major economic advantage for rural businesses and consumers.

These kinds of issues are not even brought to the attention of state regulatory commissions because no one argues the case for rural economic development in the context of a telecommunications rate setting. Regulatory commissions in many states are likely to be responsive, but are unlikely or unable to act unless the case is made in a record before them, because of the quasi-judicial nature of their proceedings.[28]

In addition to addressing the aforementioned policy questions, state policymakers and rural community leaders may wish to pursue a specific programmatic idea to link remote rural communities with vibrant urban economies. In 1985, the Swedish government created the first of what is now called rural "telecottages," which function as "A training center, library, electronic post office, dataprocessing service bureau, communications center, and a tele-shop." Nearby residents work in these telecottages on personal computers and use modems and facsimile machines to exchange information and data. Most of the work involves back-office functions such as telemarketing, customer support, filling mail orders, and data entry. The telecottage concept has been developed in New Guinea, Sri Lanka, Nigeria, India, Indonesia, and in several South American counties.[29]

Chapter 1 included the story of a housewife in Salt Lake City who answered calls, while her children were in school, that were bounced from another location to respond to a customer's question about product delivery. Indeed, the current telecommunications literature includes boundless examples of customer service calls transferred by satellite to be answered by consumer service representatives in other countries. For example, according to a 1992

Forbes article, "More than 25,000 documents a day, including credit card applications, are scanned electronically in the U.S. and copies are transmitted to Montego Bay and Kingston (Jamaica) for handling."[30]

Virtually every rural community has an underutilized room that could be outfitted with modern telecommunications equipment. It might be the community room of the library, space in the courthouse or school, or even in an

---

Box 4-3
Telecommunications in Nebraska and Nebraska Online

Nebraska is one of the leading states in its efforts to use telecommunications to strengthen its economic base and to assist development throughout the state. Omaha, for example, is often cited as one of the national centers for the telemarketing industry. This success resulted, in part, from the deregulation efforts begun in the mid-80s under Governor Kerrey and his leadership in using the purchasing power of state government to encourage the state telephone utilities to meet certain goals for providing service in the state.[31]

Nebraska has forty-two different companies serving the state, which has posed a number of problems: "They are 42 companies going in 42 different directions — building digital islands at different speeds." The state Division of Communication sponsored a retreat on June 25, 1991, attended by sixty industry representatives and forty members from state institutions. This and other efforts to facilitate discussions within the industry and coordinate future investments have made substantial progress "toward developing a statewide, open infrastructure available to everyone including the banking industry for POS and ATM services; the insurance industry for EDI and imaging technologies; and the medical community for long-distance transport of images and the provision of long-distance rural health care."[32]

Nebraska state government has also been a leader in using technology to provide direct access to information. Under an executive order by Gov. E. Benjamin Nelson, the Nebraska Development Network — which consists of a large number of partners — was formed to create and support community-based economic development. The Network, the Library Commission, and the Nebraska Rural Development Commission developed an electronic network known as Nebraska Online. This system is fully functional as a statewide information and communications tool for economic development. It is

---

abandoned building. In many circumstances, the cost of obtaining the equipment and providing appropriate training for local workers would not be prohibitive. Potential barriers to establishing such telecottages throughout rural America include an inferior level of service from the existing telephone system (in some areas), the lack of organizational capacity to coordinate such projects, and the lack of leadership to make it happen.

accessible to anyone within the state with a computer and a modem. It presents a simple menu system to access: a statewide calendar of events; jobs listings; Nebraska Development Services Directory; Nebraska Library Commission Online Catalog; electronic mail; and many federal government databases. The Library Commission is also assisting local libraries to obtain computers and modems so that this network will be available to virtually everyone throughout the state.

In displaying the Nebraska Online technology at a press conference, Governor Nelson said: "This partnership allows our businesses and communities to access the information necessary to compete in a global economy. That information is available now, and with the advent of Nebraska Online has become easily accessible to the vast majority of our citizens. This partnership will help put virtually unlimited information in the hands of Nebraskans who are attempting to reshape the future of their communities and this state." [33]

It has become a cliché that information is powerful and that access to it is extremely important. The word "empowerment" has reentered our contemporary vocabulary as an important objective for social policy. It means simply providing both information and opportunities for individuals (and, in some cases, communities as well) to make wise choices that will affect their futures. Nebraska Online "empowers" the users of this network in a way that alters the traditional relationship between clients and providers. For comparison, consider the dependency relationship inherent whenever community leaders or entrepreneurs seek information or assistance from understaffed, overburdened state agencies — information and service are given at the convenience of the providers.

As discussed in chapter 1, back-office functions are extremely mobile, although thus far English-speaking communities have had an advantage. For this reason, most of these jobs are not well compensated and, hence, lower-wage countries have a major cost advantage over the rural communities in this nation. Could telecottages in rural America provide these services competitively — in terms of cost and quality — compared with similar operations in Ireland, Jamaica, India, or elsewhere? Certainly, if there are economic or social reasons for retaining some of these back-office functions in this country, those rural communities willing to make investments in their telecommunications systems and in worker training programs would be quite competitive and would have domestic comparative advantages.

Telecommunications systems can achieve two vital objectives that will improve the competitiveness of rural economies — to establish a strong link with the urban, national, and global economies; and to improve communications and create more effective business networks within rural communities. As will be discussed later in this chapter, entrepreneurs benefit from the stimulation, ideas, and information of other entrepreneurs. For example, an old log house in Cody, Wyoming, which was once the Holiday Inn coffee shop, is now the home of the Big Horn BBS (a computer bulletin board) that serves as an electronic network for students, community leaders, and entrepreneurs throughout the region.[34]

In Walter Wriston's book, *The Twilight of Sovereignty*, he used the term "global conversation" to capture how the telephone and the computer networks are shrinking our world. He noted that every hour over 100 million telephone calls are made throughout the world using 300 million access lines. The estimated volume of phone transactions will triple by the year 2000. In reviewing Wriston's book in the *Harvard Business Review*, Alan M. Webber concluded:

> Those who are most plugged into this global conversation stand to gain the most from it. Those outside the conversation — by virtue of political ideology, personal choice, poverty, or misfortune — risk total economic failure, a fact that is as true for countries as it is for companies.[35]

Resources for Developing a Telecommunication Policy

- *Electronic Byways: State Policies for Rural Development Through Telecommunications*, Edwin B. Parker et al. (Boulder, Colo.: Westview Press/Aspen Institute, 1992).

- *New Alliances in Innovation: A Guide to Encouraging Innovative Applications of New Communication Technologies to Address State Problems*, Nancy Ginn

Helme, (Washington, D.C.: Council of Governors' Policy Advisors, 1993).

- *Rural America at the Crossroads: Networking for the Future*, U.S. Congress, Office of Technology Assessment (OTA-TCT-471), April 1991. Available from the Superintendent of Documents, U.S. Government Printing Office, Washington, D.C. 20402-9325.

- *State and Local Tax Policy and the Telecommunication Industry*, Karl E. Case, (Washington, D.C.: Council of Governors' Policy Advisors, 1993).

- *Telecomm '92: Connecting Idaho to the Future*, A Strategic Plan for Idaho Telecommunications, Lloyd Howe and Dick Gardner, Project Managers, Department of Administration, Capitol Building, Boise, Idaho 83720-1000, 208.334.3900.

Promoting Entrepreneurship

The word "entrepreneur" was first used by Jean Baptiste Say almost two centuries ago to define a person who "shifts economic resources out of an area of lower and into an area of higher productivity and greater yield." [36] Although the word is often associated with people who start their own businesses or who take risks, Peter Drucker's book, *Innovation and Entrepreneurship: Practices and Principles* provided numerous examples of individuals and organizations exploiting opportunities and moving resources to more productive, higher uses. He expressed tempered optimism about the American economy — despite its challenges — because entrepreneurship and innovation have been so pervasive throughout our society. He noted that, "It is still too early to say whether the entrepreneurial economy will remain primarily an American phenomenon or whether it will emerge in other industrially developed countries.... So far, the entrepreneurial economy is purely an American phenomenon." [37]

Published in the same year as Drucker's book (1985), *The Wealth of States* argued that state development policy should promote entrepreneurship, instead of recruitment, and provided three reasons:

- It encourages diversification, so that local economies do not become dependent on a single firm or industry.

- Existing state residents are not forced to bear the direct and indirect costs of subsidies to recruit or retain industry from outside the state.

- Entrepreneurs and their backers, and not the community at large, bear the risk of failure.

Most of its policy recommendations related to removing barriers to entry and exit in regulated businesses or professions, to reforming state policies that limited competition, and to streamlining the environmental, health, and other regulations with which businesses must comply.[38] These remain laudable strategies for state governments.

This book made another observation that aids in understanding the challenge of promoting rural competitiveness: "Those states or communities that have been dominated for decades by a single industry or firm paying high wages have not had the opportunity to develop an entrepreneurial tradition."[39] The lack of entrepreneurial tradition has been a social disadvantage in many poor, disadvantaged communities — especially those dominated by a single industry or firm. Diversified economies provide more business opportunities than are found in the stereotypical company town, and they also provide more entrepreneurs who serve as role models for everyone in the community.

An entrepreneurial culture is one in which individuals and organizations pursue opportunities that produce wealth, innovation, and quality improvements. The task of promoting, nurturing, and developing entrepreneurship in both the private and public sectors is an elusive, but important, objective for state and local governments. Fostering an entrepreneurial culture in rural economies reliant upon a few dominant industries may be an even greater challenge. Dr. Alan S. Gregerman has produced a simple matrix for Assessing Your Community's Entrepreneurial Environment (see box 4-4) that serves an important reminder that key elements of communities can contribute to providing a supportive culture of innovation, flexibility, and collective responses to economic challenges.

In their study of Silicon Valley, Everett Rogers and Judith Larsen captured the importance of the entrepreneurial tradition, the value of these role models, and the powerful magnets they become:

> The most important single factor in the rise of a "Silicon Valley" is entrepreneurial fever. It is doubtful that its spirit can be taught in formal classes, although several universities now have courses on entrepreneurship. *Entrepreneurship is best learned by example.* When individuals know of successful role models like Steve Jobs, Bob Noyce, Bill Hewlett, Dave Packard, and Nolan Bushnell, they naturally begin to think, "If he did it, why can't I?" Once an entrepreneurial climate becomes established in an area like Silicon Valley, individuals seek work there in order to step into an entrepreneurial role. Entrepreneurial fever is concentrated in an area both by modeling and by selective migration. (Emphasis added.)[40]

Box 4-4

Assessing Your Community's Entrepreneurial Environment

Element/Component	STRENGTHS		LIMITATIONS	
	Major	Minor	Minor	Major
1. Leadership				
Inspiring Vision of the Future				
Broad Local Support				
Longer-term Perspective				
Culture of Cooperation				
Bias toward Action				
Cheerleading from the Start				
2. Talent				
Pool of Successful Entrepreneurs				
Skilled Work Force				
Strong Network of Professionals				
Appropriate Technical Expertise				
3. Opportunities				
Entrepreneurial Education				
Marketplace Information				
Resource Base Information				
Partners				
Development Facilities				
4. Innovation				
Corporations				
Colleges or Universities				
Public Nonprofit Institutions				
5. Capital				
Seed and Equity Capital				
Affordable Debt Financing				
6. Spirit				
Civic Pride and Image				
Quality of Life				
Supportive and Involved Media				

Source: Alan S. Gregerman, "Rekindling the Future," *Commentary*; (Winter 1991).

The low population density of rural communities and their reliance upon a few dominant industries might suggest that enterprise development is an uncommon phenomenon. Mark Popovich, the primary author of several case studies of rural entrepreneurship during the 1980s, has found much more rural entrepreneurship than one might expect:

> Contrary to the common stereotype, many rural economies are indeed dynamic. Some of the country's hardest-pressed rural areas — persistent poverty counties of Arkansas's Mississippi Delta and the oil and gas "bust belt" of western North Dakota — are keeping pace with their urbanized counterparts in generating jobs through new enterprise development. While many rural families face severe financial stress, hundreds of thousands of others are succeeding in creating new enterprises. These businesses almost always start out small. But when their total impact is weighed, their role in sparking income and employment opportunities becomes clear.[41]

Using standard data sources and surveys of new business owners, Popovich and his colleagues compared enterprise development in rural counties in Arkansas, Iowa, Maine, and North Dakota. Here are his major conclusions:

- Successful new businesses made a significant contribution to these four rural state's economies. Employment generated by new businesses is an important influence on all four of these statewide economies.

- Entrepreneurship is alive and well in rural communities as they kept pace with their urban counterparts in benefiting from the jobs attributed to new businesses.

- New businesses can be found in all major industrial sectors. However, as is true of the national economy as a whole, the employment generated by successfully formed new businesses tends to increase the importance of the services, retail trade, and wholesale trade sectors.

- New businesses have proved to be surprisingly durable — both overall in these rural states and in their rural counties. Survival rates appear to be much higher than previous studies of new business survival rates would suggest.[42]

Popovich reported that most rural businesses were homegrown; new business owners had diverse backgrounds, but many are younger and better educated than the average community resident; *women, minorities, and the poor were underrepresented* (emphasis added); most owners had positive motivations in starting their business; most were not experienced entrepreneurs; most new businesses were started from scratch, relying heavily upon family members; although starting small, most generated employment growth; most new rural businesses had obtained start-up financing from a local lender, although personal savings, deferred wages, and family loans were also important; and, despite low participation rates, the rural businesses that did participate in business assistance programs rated them highly.[43] (See box 4-5 for Popovich's recommendations for state business development assistance programs.)

Several of his recommendations for state business development assistance programs have been tested by various states in recent years. The questions of scale and design for small business assistance programs merit additional attention. The SBA Small Business Development Centers must provide services to every applicant who walks into their offices. Are those applicants more likely than other entrepreneurs to succeed and generate employment with their business venture? Should business assistance be targeted in some manner to serve those most likely to succeed? How much business assistance could or should public-sector agencies (either state or federal) provide to a particular firm? What are the public benefits from assisting an entrepreneur to start a new business that competes directly with existing, established firms? Should fees be charged for these services?

Small business assistance programs could be rationalized and their service delivery systems redesigned in various ways — by sector, by employment potential, by applicants, or by price. The sectoral approach would limit business assistance to new and small enterprises active in strategically advantageous industries such as value-added secondary products from natural resources. The employment potential approach would limit assistance to new and small businesses with the greatest potential for generating jobs. The applicant approach would limit assistance to those entrepreneurs who, owing to gender, race, or ethnicity, have had less opportunity through traditional institutions to start new businesses. And the price approach would charge a fee for the business assistance.

Each of these screening devices is theoretically plausible, but has proved to be difficult to achieve through public-sector agencies. This may explain the reason that most state enterprise development programs provide limited assistance to virtually all those who request it. Providing a higher quality of business services to selective entrepreneurs could be more effective than the current practice, but how would one define strategically advantageous industries? How would one assess the employment potential of a new or small business? Can the equity rationale for limiting special business assistance to

Box 4-5
Recommendations for Business Development Assistance

- Convene a council of public and private organizations involved in providing assistance to new businesses.

- Make business assistance programs more accessible to new businesses (i.e., expanded outreach efforts, a catalogue of services, clearinghouse referral system, training programs and seminars at night, use video and audio materials for training, utilize telecommunications to provide more services).

- Building marketing skills will be one of the keys to success (i.e., provide effective marketing plans, include new products in trade shows, provide catalogues and computer listings of state products).

- Create a comprehensive technology deployment service that can meet the emerging needs of new businesses.

- State efforts to expand the financing options for new businesses should focus on working in partnership with existing local lenders.

- Develop a business aspirations program to encourage small and new businesses, and the development of innovative products and services (i.e., award programs to recognize new businesses or new products: the "Governor's State Entrepreneur of the Year Award"; develop media strategy to focus positive attention on entrepreneurship in local communities or statewide; promote business and school-based efforts to train entrepreneurs; and provide newsletters to new and small businesses with useful information about market trends, regulatory responsibilities, technological applications and business management ideas).

- Use the flexibility provided by the Family Support Act to encourage aid recipients to seek greater independence through self-employment or by starting their own business.

Source: Mark G. Popovich, *New Businesses, Entrepreneurship and Rural Development: State Policies and Generating Rural Growth from Within*, Final Project Report to the Ford Foundation, (Washington, D.C.: Council of Governors' Policy Advisors, 1993), 34-38.

narrowly defined categories of entrepreneurs be clearly articulated, and will the public support the preference policy?

The strongest argument for rationalizing business assistance programs is through price, preferably with sliding scale fees. One of the best programs established by women to assist other women get started in business is the Women's Economic Development Corporation (WEDCO) in St. Paul, Minnesota. If the advice provided by WEDCO is good enough for a bank to finance its clients, then a fee is charged. These fees cover about one-third of the organization's budget and constitute a very strong incentive to provide high-quality assistance. From an institutional perspective, small business centers may not be as oriented toward results (at least as much as WEDCO is) "because the quality of technical assistance is not linked to their budgets." [44]

State business assistance programs could be more effectively coordinated with the services provided by federal agencies and local governments. Some basic information and business services could be provided to all who request assistance. Charging a fee for higher quality business services, such as marketing advice and developing business plans, provides a higher form of accountability on the service delivery system — and a superior use of public funds.

Assisting small businesses has been a popular economic development strategy for several years, beginning with David Birch's observations that small businesses accounted for most of the employment growth during the 1970s. Unfortunately, small business advocates and many economic development officials have failed to appreciate the significance of Birch's research. David Osborne has clarified this important misperception:

> Small-business advocates have pushed the study so hard that it has become identified with the thesis that small business is the key to economic development. In reality, as Birch himself as often stressed, the real lesson is that innovation, which often happens in young, growing firms, is the key to economic development. Most small firms are irrelevant; they feed off growth, rather than creating it.[45]

In the absence of an ability by the public sector to identify and target special assistance to innovative firms, simply providing services to new businesses that compete against existing businesses may produce limited economic development benefits. As currently designed, the small business service strategy suffers from a lack of clarity about its public purpose and an infrequent evaluation of its social benefits.

Nevertheless, promoting entrepreneurship serves important social objectives: for individuals, it provides economic opportunity; for communities, it encourages organizations to accept, embrace, and shape change. Both are important to economic development. Promoting small businesses is a particularly important economic development strategy for rural communities. As economic development expert William Nothdurft explained:

> Unlike the much sought-after branch plants or footloose industries, local businesses have a vested interest in the community, purchase supplies locally, participate in community affairs and, because they are part of the community, are less likely to lay off employees or move on when times get tough. They are stakeholders in the community.[46]

Resources for Promoting Entrepreneurship

- Dr. Alan S. Gregerman, VENTURE WORKS, Inc., Silver Spring, Maryland, (who assists local governments and corporations in creating environments for entrepreneurs).

- William E. Nothdurft, *Going Global: How Europe Helps Small Firms Export*, (Brookings Institution, Washington, D.C., 1992).

- Peter F. Drucker, *Innovation and Entrepreneurship: Practice and Principles*, (Harper and Row, New York, 1986).

- *New Business, Entrepreneurship and Rural Development: State Policies and Generating Rural Growth from Within, and The Wealth of States, and 101 Ideas for Stimulating Rural Entrepreneurship and New Business Development*: Council of Governors' Policy Advisors, Suite 390, 400 North Capitol, Washington, D.C. 20001; 202.624.5386.

- "Promoting Small Business: Lessons for Technical Assistance Providers and Others," Northwest Report (November 1990); A Newsletter of the Northwest Area Foundation, 322 Minnesota Street, Suite E-1201, St. Paul, Minnesota 55101-1373; 612.224.9635.

Access to Capital

Rural communities and innercity neighborhoods are two geographic places that often are denied effective access to capital for enterprise development. The three most important reasons are chronic poverty, traditional discrimination, and lack of institutional lenders concerned about those specific geographic areas. Some rural communities and inner-city neighborhoods are so chronically poor that very little private capital is readily available. These capital-poor areas are so plagued by high risk that private capital is quite scarce, even for supremely qualified borrowers. The degree of the associated risk affects the premium attached to the cost of capital. Yet, relatively few communities and neighborhoods are so poverty-stricken that simply no capital is available, at any price, to anyone, for any purpose.

Most rural communities and inner-city neighborhoods — even poor ones — have modest amounts of private capital, but preferential access to that capital is given to established firms, members of prominent families, qualified borrowers with long banking histories, and those of the majority culture and the male gender. The effect of these traditional practices severely limits access to capital for younger, higher-risk entrepreneurs, members of minority groups, and female applicants. Equal opportunity is not the typical standard for allocating credit in many, and perhaps most, communities.

The final problem occurs whenever a community or neighborhood lacks financial institutions that are concerned about the future viability of the area. In a study of the South Shore Bank, Richard Taub noted that this community — even during the 1970s when housing was declining and storefronts were being closed — always had some savings, but it was being placed, for various reasons, mostly into the large banks downtown. Needless to add, those larger banks had little interest in making small business loans or home mortgages in the South Shore community. The diminishing capital investment in the community accelerated its decline. Even though the South Shore community in Chicago was becoming much poorer, it still had capital in the form of private savings; what it lacked were the community institutions such as the South Shore Bank to serve its capital needs, to maintain the community's social and economic viability.[47]

One of the best descriptions of the importance of capital in rural development was written by Patrick J. Sullivan of the Economic Research Service:

> The availability of affordable financial capital has long been recognized as an important factor in economic growth and development. Many firms and governments rely on borrowed funds to help finance their daily operations, and few have the resources to finance significant expansion of their capital solely with current revenues and retained earnings. With adequate financing, businesses and governments can adjust to market and technological developments in ways that improve the productivity of local resources. If external funding is not available, or is available at prohibitively high costs, investment in productive capital and infrastructure might have to be postponed or canceled, depressing the area's future economic

growth. Access to debt and equity capital markets is, therefore, necessary for sustained economic development within modern economies.[48]

The perception of private market imperfection or failures has been used as the rationale for public-sector financing programs for small or new businesses. The conventional argument is that:

Small firms in markets served by large banks, and large firms in markets served by small banks are often dissatisfied with their local financial institutions. Firms involved in unfamiliar technologies or product lines...experience relatively high loan denial rates. Newly starting firms and rapidly expanding firms have more problems acquiring financing than do stable, well-established firms.[49]

Some analysts have suggested that the rationale for public-sector programs to provide small business lending is stronger now than in the past and cite three reasons:

- The banking industry restructured during the 1980s, which consolidated many banks and allowed larger banks to branch into small communities, placing more competitive pressure on the remaining smaller banks;

- After the savings and loan industry collapse, regulators began to scrutinize closely the exposure of smaller institutions, which has restricted credit to smaller businesses; and

- The Federal Deposit Insurance Corporation Improvement Act of 1991 "will mean higher costs, and make small business lending more challenging."[50]

Because of low population density, many rural communities lack a wide range of financial institutions from which to choose. This lack of choice does not — by itself— mean that most entrepreneurs suffer from inadequate or inappropriate banking services. Indeed, one recent study concluded that "The available evidence suggests that the vast majority of rural nonfarm businesses are satisfied with their financial service providers, particularly for short- and medium-term credit." [51] It is likely, however, that the lack of choice for banking services in rural communities has the greatest negative impact on potential entrepreneurs, female or minority applicants, small business owners, firms involved in unfamiliar technologies or product lines, or new ventures.

State governments have adopted several strategies in responding to perceived market imperfections. Rural town and county governments, for example, often are denied access to the established bond markets because of their small size and lack of credit rating. In response to this problem, Illinois, Vermont, Maine, and several other states have established State Bond Banks to consolidate the bonding needs of these local governments and issue larger bonds with the state's credit rating.

State governments have issued regulations designed to encourage or require financial institutions to meet the capital needs of their communities.[52] Regulations in most states prohibit racial discrimination by state-regulated financial institutions, although it continues to be a serious problem in most parts of the country. In their book, *Credit Where It's Due*, Parzen and Kieschnick noted that "New York has a community-reinvestment act that offers new real-estate-investment powers to commercial banks based upon their community-reinvestment performance." And they cited the proposal of the commerce commissioner in Minnesota to expand "community-reinvestment standards to include life-insurance and securities firms and making public ratings of financial institutions based on their service to communities."[53]

Linked deposits are popular with state governments in encouraging bank lending to meet critical capital needs. A state invests part of its portfolio, at below market interest rates, in a bank — if the latter agrees to make loans in underserved communities or to loan to small businesses. This may be a good strategy for directing public capital toward underserved communities, but the strategy often fails when directed at small businesses. Here is the analysis by Markley and McKee from their book *Business Finance as a Tool for Development*:

> Since in most cases the small business borrower already qualifies for a market-rate loan, the linked deposit program simply results in an interest subsidy. Moreover, the state sacrifices revenues on its deposits, anticipating that the public benefits — increased tax revenues and employment from business expansion — will compensate for the loss. The results show mixed performance depending on the types of loans made and the targeting of the program. One study of six state-linked deposit programs found that the states, on average, lost about $4,000 per loan. Since the programs were not targeted explicitly to groups with capital access problems, the economic development benefits were nebulous.[54]

These authors strongly recommend the Massachusetts linked-deposit approach to assisting development in targeted, underserved communities. Any bank or thrift in the state can bid for state deposits but, as a condition of the award, they must "allocate 70 percent to specified kinds of loans, such as small business loans, mortgages and home improvement loans *in low-income commu-*

nities or neighborhoods" (emphasis added).[55] This superior approach directs public capital to fill the gaps among targeted groups in underserved areas.

Most state economic development agencies administer loan programs for small businesses and some provide venture capital to new firms. As evidenced by the performance of the federal Small Business Administration, public-sector lending is often a difficult balancing act. Granting loans to the pool of applicants who were rejected by private lenders carries inherently high risks. Deliberate screening and prudent lending reduces risks, but might supplant the lending being done by the private sector and stray from the agency's mission. Furthermore, these programs often mistakenly subsidize the loans by offering below-market interest rates. As a general rule, *the priority concern for any public intervention strategy should be to increase the availability of capital to all qualified borrowers, not to subsidize the cost of capital to a few applicants.*[56] In addition, some of these public programs have not been designed to target firms or applicants according to specific criteria to promote economic development objectives (for example, loaning to a new or struggling retail shop is less likely to stimulate new employment than lending to a firm ready to expand its operation).

A broader critique of these traditional approaches to development finance by public-sector agencies came from a 1989 study by David Osborne:

> After a decade of innovation in development finance, the record is quite mixed.... More often than not, however, states still create small public funds rather than seeking to change what happens in the marketplace. They retail their public money, rather than using it wholesale — to change private investment patterns.
>
> At times, to hit particular niches, retailing is necessary. But because the typical public fund has only about $10 million in capital, retailing strategies that are not aimed at very small niches have had marginal impact. They also have been susceptible to political pressures from legislatures and governors' offices, leading them at times to make poor investment decisions.[57]

State governments have continued to innovate in the field of development finance as active investors and as passive investors, often by creating new organizational entities. Here is a sample of the approaches described by Markley and McKee:

- Minnesota created the Community Reinvestment Fund to serve as a financial intermediary for community development corporations and municipalities.

The CRF sells community reinvestment revenue bonds to private investors and purchases loans made by community development corporations and municipal governments.

- Michigan created Business and Industrial Development Corporations, which are private financial institutions designed to provide moderate-risk capital with the initial public investment matched 2 to 1 by private capital. One of these is a Rural BIDCO, which along with a Minority BIDCO, received greater public subsidies from the state.

- Many states have revolving loan funds to meet "capital needs that are too small or too risky for banks to meet" when investment is perceived to be likely to generate social or economic development benefits.

- Illinois uses a direct lending program to provide subordinated debt financing to small business. The state funds, limited to up to 25 percent of each loan, "act like a second mortgage for the borrower and increase the chances of private financing."

In addition, the authors also emphasized the importance of providing technical assistance to businesses along with these financing approaches and described the fine work of the Northern Economic Initiatives Center as a model for providing these services.[58]

Three other approaches merit attention for state policymakers concerned about the lack of capital availability in rural communities and its significance for economic development — development banks, microenterprise lending, and revolving loan funds. Parzen and Kieschnick define the former:

> Financial institutions created primarily to foster economic development are development banks. As financial institutions, they seek to conserve their capital; as development vehicles, they seek to contribute to economic development. Development banks must be both sustainable financial institutions and cost-effective development vehicles, and these roles sometimes conflict.[59]

These authors identified several examples of development banks serving various important functions in rural settings. They mentioned the Northern Community Investment Corporation in St. Johnsbury, Vermont, that is involved in business financing and real estate development; the Southern Development Bancorporation in Arkansas (formed with the assistance of Shorebank Corporation), which was established to fill gaps in the availability of capital in rural communities; and the Blackfeet National Bank in Browning, Montana, (formed by the Blackfeet tribe). They also discussed how different forms of financial institutions could serve as development banks.[60]

Another promising approach to expand the availability of capital in rural communities is called microenterprise development or microlending. The model for this approach is the Grameen Bank in Bangladesh, which began in 1976 "to test the effectiveness of supplying the poor with working capital as a means to self-employment and, ultimately, to poverty alleviation." It began small, as a one-person operation. Within two years, it was lending to fewer than 100 borrowers. But, by 1987, the bank had almost 300 branches and had assisted nearly 250 thousand households. Most loans are very small and go to landless women. The default rate is less than 2 percent. Last year, it lent more than $70 million to 700 thousand borrowers.[61]

Since the mid-1980s, more than one hundred microenterprise loan funds have been established in this country with funding from foundations, government, and nonprofit organizations that serve community needs. Typically, microenterprise refers "to very small businesses operating from a home, storefront, or office that employ fewer than five people, frequently only one person," although USIA and other international organizations define microenterprises as having fewer than ten employees. These businesses tend to be in the retail and service sectors, require modest amounts of start-up capital, and "invariably lack access to conventional sources of credit and capital because of their modest size, lack of collateral, insufficient equity, and management inexperience." Indeed, as a point of reference for the significance of microenterprise lending, it is significant to note that "approximately 78% of all small businesses were started with less than $5,000 in capital," according to the Small Business Administration's report: *1982 Characteristics of Small Business Owners.*[62]

In so short a time, microenterprise lending has demonstrated striking potential in assisting targeted groups, especially women, that have traditionally had little or no access to conventional lenders to gain self-employment and start small businesses. According to Martin Connell, president of the Calmeadow Foundation, "There is a growing realization that this type of vehicle (microenterprise lending) is more effective in unlocking human potential than the use of charitable gifts." [63] Indeed, one measure of the potential of this strategy was its rapid adoption as a pilot program by the federal Small Business Administration. Authorized by a 1991 appropriations amendment, SBA announced it would provide $15 million in loans and grants to 35 nonprofit organizations in thirty states, which would use these funds to make "microloans" targeted to poor, minority, and female entrepreneurs.[64]

The best summary of the current debate about the viability of microenterprise loan funds as an economic development strategy is presented in a report prepared by the Shorebank Advisory Services, Inc. for, and published by, the Charles Stewart Mott Foundation. This is an excellent resource that should prove to be valuable for state policymakers and rural community leaders (noted below under resources). Even if this approach fails to fulfill the ambitious claims of its champions, it could nevertheless expand economic and social opportunities to many people not well served by existing financial institutions.

As discussed, the availability of capital for business expansion, new ventures, small businesses, and entrepreneurs is critical to maintain the viability of rural economies. Rural communities often do not have many choices about where to obtain banking services. In addition, traditional banking practices have sometimes limited the availability of credit to selective applicants and to established firms in dominant sectors. These circumstances may justify state intervention in rural financial markets, which could take the form of state regulations, linked deposits, BIDCOs, revolving loan funds, direct lending, development banks, or microenterprise lending programs.

Before developing policy in this area, however, state governments may wish to undertake two interim steps: an objective study of actual capital gaps in rural communities and a series of education and training workshops. Rural advocates often allege that credit is categorically denied to rural communities, and they cite the aforementioned reasons. A survey indicating that most existing businesses are satisfied with current banking services within the community provides little information about those who are being denied credit and whether that is justified or arbitrary. Sometimes, however, the lack of banking lending within a rural community reflects the lack of demand for credit. It is quite difficult to assess real, as distinct from perceived, capital gaps in targeted geographic areas.

An objective study of the actual capital gap in rural communities is recommended because it can guide state policymakers to design the most appropriate and effective public intervention. For example, the amount of public capital devoted to small business development in some communities may already be greater than is generally perceived. The National Association of Development Organizations (NADO) conducted a survey in December 1992 of over 300 revolving loan funds administered by economic development districts and other regional development organizations across the country. These revolving loan funds were capitalized by the U.S. Economic Development Agency (EDA) under the Title IX program. Below is the summary of survey results:

The 94 respondents had over $73 million from EDA in their revolving loan funds. In addition, the RLFs had numerous other sources of capital, including: Rural Development Administration (RDA), Health and Human Services (HHS), Appalachian Regional Commission (ARC), Housing and Urban Development (HUD), as well as state and local funds. All sources together contributed more than $170.5 million.[65]

Many states have used federal Community Development Grant Funds to create revolving loan funds as well. In addition, the Clinton administration's proposed 1994 budget included $60 million to create a network of community banks, presumably modeled after the successful Southern Development Bancorporation in Arkansas, "to provide loans for business and housing purposes in distressed communities that have previously been underserved by traditional lending institutions." [66] The policy debate has, apparently, progressed from addressing whether public capital should be provided to assist community economic development to the question of how the provision of public capital to communities should be organized and structured.

An objective study of the credit problem of rural communities is helpful for another reason as well. Much has been learned about development finance during the past decade, but the evaluations of many of these programs are often inconclusive about their net public benefit. For example, in evaluating the performance of a public loan program, researchers should be asking whether it supplanted the loans normally made by private institutions or provided capital to those previously denied access to it. If it serves primarily the former function, then the intervention provides little public benefit. But if it serves the latter function, it may indeed provide some public benefit.

The other interim step that state policymakers may wish to consider is to conduct a series of education and training programs in rural communities on business finance topics for both: bankers and entrepreneurs (current and potential ones). Most small business development centers provide information about credit and financing arrangements to small business owners and those considering starting new ventures, although there may be new and better ways — such as through telecommunications systems or business networks — to disseminate this information widely. Rural bankers should also be identified and targeted as key people who could be given additional information and training about how to evaluate the risk of innovative or unconventional business loans.

Two of the states that participated in the CGPA's 1990 State Policy Academy on Rural Economic and Community Development — Iowa and North Dakota — developed continuing education programs for community bank lenders to facilitate the availability of financing for small and new businesses. In North Dakota, the program was sponsored by the Bank of North Dakota, the Department of Economic Development, the Bankers' Association, the Independent Bankers' Association, and local development organizations. In Iowa, workshops on making nonagricultural loans were held in cooperation with the Iowa Bankers' Association and attended by more than two hundred bankers. Educating rural lenders about nontraditional business needs may be a low-cost means of expanding the availability of credit in some rural communities. Similarly, community leaders who have perceived unmet credit needs locally have sought to educate urban bankers about potential rural markets.

Resources for Increasing Access to Capital

- *Business Finance as a Tool for Development*, Deborah Markley with Katherine McKee, The Aspen Institute, 1333 New Hampshire Ave. NW, Suite 1070, Washington, D.C. 20036; 202-736-5800.

- *Community Capital Builders: A Leadership Brief on Rural Intermediaries and Rural Intermediary Funding Act: A Policy Brief and Model Legislation*, Center for Policy Alternatives, 1875 Connecticut Ave. N.W., Suite 710, Washington, D.C. 20009; 202.387.6030.

- *Credit Where It's Due: Development Banking for Communities*, Julia Ann Parzen and Michael Hall Kieschnick, Temple University Press, Philadelphia, Pa. 19122.

- *Financial Market Intervention as a Rural Development Strategy*, Agriculture and Rural Economy Division, Economic Research Service, USDA, February 1990, Washington, D.C. 20005-4788; Copies available from ERS-NASS, P.O.Box 1608, Rockville, Md. 20849-1608; 1.800.999.6779.

- *Hopeful Change: The Potential of Micro-enterprise Programs as a Community Revitalization Intervention*, Jacqueline Novogratz, The Rockefeller Foundation, 1133 Avenue of the Americas, New York, N.Y. 10036; 212.869.8500.

- "Self-Employment Learning Project," Margaret E. Clark, Director, The Aspen Institute, 1333 New Hampshire Avenue, N.W., Suite 1070, Washington, D.C. 20036; 202.736.5800.

- *Widening The Window of Opportunity: Strategies for the Evolution of Microenterprise Loan Funds*, Prepared by Shorebank Advisory Services, Inc., Commissioned and Published by the Charles Stewart Mott Foundation, 1200 Mott Foundation Building, Flint, Mich. 48502-1851; 313.238.5651.

Natural Resources Development

The nation is blessed with bountiful natural resources, and throughout our history they have provided the source of much of the wealth for rural communities. According to William Nothdurft:

> Natural resources play a dual role in the creation of (state) comparative advantages. They create opportunities for new and expanded businesses, and they establish, or can be used to establish, the state's amenity values as powerful magnets for new growth. Climate, available freshwater, coastline, energy resources, forests, prime agricultural lands, all contribute to both advantages.[67]

Many states have developed new initiatives to "enhance the productivity of resource assets, to enhance the expansion of natural resource-based primary industries and the birth of new natural resource enterprises."[68] A summary of the state goals in resource-related development in California, Alaska, Maine, Montana, and other states is presented in box 4-6.

The state role has been greatest in agriculture. For example, in a survey of state strategies for promoting agricultural exports, Mark Popovich described three main categories:

- *Helping the sellers* by generating trade leads and building the skills needed to succeed;

- *Reaching the buyers* through trade shows and other alternatives;

- *Developing the market* by identifying new marketing opportunities and assisting firms in product development or refinement.[69]

States have helped firms market products, especially food and handicrafts, by emphasizing quality. Vermont has a Seal of Quality label that is given to quality food products. Maine has a state label that is used primarily for handicrafts and small wood products. Wisconsin cheeses proudly wear its label. Kona coffee and Macadamia nuts are known for their Hawaiian origin. Many of the southern and southwestern states compete to produce the world's best barbecue sauce, and who could forget the Idaho potato? The latter maintains such a strong public image because the state's potato industry directs an annual $5 million national advertising campaign.[70]

Another prominent strategy is to capture within the state some of the value-added components of the raw commodities that are grown, harvested, mined, or cut before they are exported to urban or global markets. The objec-

Box 4-6
State Goals for Resource-related Development

Maximizing sustainable resource yield: that is ensuring that available resources are managed and used in ways that enhance their long-term productivity — extending the life of nonrenewable resources through efficient extraction and maximum recycling, and sustaining rather than consuming renewable resource assets;

Increasing reliance on renewable resources: helping the market to increase projects and programs designed to accelerate the commercialization of renewable resource-based technologies and industries, but not necessarily to replace nonrenewable-based industries but to provide the full range of efficient choice and to insulate the state from the effects of declining supplies of nonrenewable factors of production;

Enhancing environmental quality: enhancing not simply for its own sake but to attract and retain profitable, job-generating economic activity and ensure public health and safety;

Increasing stability and self-reliance: increasing not to achieve "independence," a goal impossible to attain at the national, much less state, level, but to provide some measure of protection from external fluctuations in the supply and price of resources critical to economic activity;

Reducing economic waste: by removing, where possible, subsidies, tax policies, and regulations that price valuable resources cheaply and disguise their true production costs and by encouraging efficient use of material inputs to production; and

Improving value-added: helping to guarantee that maximum economic value is received within the state from the use of the state's natural resource assets.

Source: William E. Nothdurft, *Renewing America: Natural Resource Assets and State Economic Development*, (Washington, D.C.: CSPA, 1984), 167-168.

tive is to retain the product development process within the state, capturing the wealth and employment associated with these processes. The state of Maine, for example, has recognized that the value of the fish landed can be increased seven times through processing, packaging, and marketing functions. It has sought to capture these value-added functions by providing technical and business management assistance to the small enterprises engaged in these functions.[71] Similarly, Oregon, Washington, Michigan, and Maine are the leaders in state initiatives to capture the value-added functions of the forestry industry by assisting enterprises that produce secondary wood products.

Oregon's approach may serve as a model for other states. In 1989 the legislature created a special interim committee on Forest Products Policy to develop a response to the crisis in the state's wood products industry. According to Joseph Cortright, who works for the legislature, the committee "hired the Northwest Policy Center of the University of Washington to conduct a series of focus groups of firm owners to identify the industry's competitive problems and opportunities." The committee then evaluated various strategies to increase the competitiveness of the state's value-added wood products producers and adopted these five criteria for subsequent state action:

1. Work with existing firms in the industry, and not focus on recruiting;

2. Allow the assistance to the industry to be led and controlled by the firms from the industry;

3. Channel efforts to recognize the diversity of firms in the industry;

4. Help firms be competitive and not dictate product or market strategies; and

5. Intervene on sufficiently adequate scale to make a difference.

Based on these criteria and the committee's recommendations, the legislature enacted a Wood Products Competitiveness Corporation, which was given broad powers including "the ability to assist the creation of industry associations, a charge to encourage the development of flexible manufacturing networks, contract for the operation of a technology extension service to help firms adopt proven technologies, and the authority to issue vouchers for services." (Note the broad powers reflect the Third Wave principles advocated by Friedman and Ross, see chapter 3.)[72]

Most states have initiated efforts to capture the value-added components from their raw commodities. Some of these efforts have included providing assistance to firms seeking to export their goods and products (see box 4-7). Emphasizing natural resource assets and the opportunities to capture the value-added production process are among the most promising avenues for promot-

Box 4-7
Regional, Sectoral Help for "Export Ready" Small Firms

Conclusions from *Going Global: How Europe Helps Small Firms Export:*

1. Everyone wants to increase small firms exports and everyone finds it difficult to do so. Officials of successful European public and private programs concede that small firms are hard to reach and hard to help, but the Europeans work hard at the problem.

2. Targeting is crucial. Deep and specific assistance provided to a small clientele will do more than shallow and vague assistance to a large one. Trade development happens one deal at a time. The most promising export assistance programs are those that provide very deep assistance to individual firms, including identification of trade partners and brokering deals.

3. Whatever large or small resources are available should be focused on firms that will help themselves. Focus on export-ready and/or export-willing firms that have sufficient management maturity to develop competent strategic plans and make a tangible financial commitment to export market development.

4. Understanding the difference between export promotion and export market development is central to creating world-class international trade programs. The focus on market development is what distinguishes the most imaginative export assistance in Europe. These programs help firms to anticipate, respond to or create overseas markets not only for existing products but for other products they could produce.

5. Just as exporting must be part of a company's overall strategic plan for growth, export development must be part of a state's or nation's overall economic competitiveness strategy. Small firm export assistance programs in Europe are typically part of a broad and coherent national competitiveness strategy, integrating export policy with technology policy, training policy and education policy.

Source: Economic Development Abroad, vol.6 no.6 (September 1992) Published by National Council for Urban Economic Development and International Center, Academy for State and Local Government; CUED, 1730 K St. NW, Washington, D.C. 20006; See William E. Nothdurft, *Going Global: How Europe Helps Small Firms Export* (Washington, D.C.: The Brookings Institution, 1992).

ing rural competitiveness. One of the best reports on this topic is *Recouple — Natural Resource Strategies for Rural Economic Development* by Midwest Research Institute, which concluded:

> We found that community-based economic development organizations do not usually focus on natural resource-based strategies. It is often assumed that the "old" natural resource primary industries — agriculture, forestry, mining and fishing — are part of the rural problem. And, in one sense, they are — rural areas have paid a price for overdependency on any one aspect of the resource base when changes in global demand, or technological change, or resource depletion have radically altered the industry and thereby the rural economy.... Lack of diversification — failing to support a broad base of employment and income-generating sectors — has been at the heart of the problem.[73]

However, the report added this cautionary note:

> Natural resources are a key asset for rural economic development. But any decision that does not take into account the need to ensure their renewability through a sustainable use strategy is indeed short-sighted. Resource conservation and management, not exploitation, are the keys to long-term sustainability of not only the natural resource base but the very fiber of our rural economies. "Ecological economics" must come to guide our decisions on our resources, and stewardship must replace development as a mission.[74]

As discussed in chapter 1, the rural landscape itself constitutes an important comparative advantage for economic development. Beginning with the successful "I Love New York" campaign in 1977, virtually every state and numerous regional and local jurisdictions have chosen to pursue tourism as an economic development strategy. Many economic development practitioners and civic leaders regard the tourist industry as clean, easy to cultivate, and growing. Indeed, one industry study estimated that tourism in 1988 "accounted for nearly 6.5 percent of the Nation's gross national product (GNP), directly generated over 5.5 million jobs, and contributed an estimated $36.6 billion in Federal, State and local tax revenues."[75]

Tourism is an enticing strategy because it is often viewed as a benign way of increasing local employment and capturing local expenditures from outside sources. Successful tourism campaigns in moderation do achieve those objectives. State policymakers should address these questions, however: Who benefits directly or indirectly from the tourist industry? What kinds of employment does it generate? Are rural regions sufficiently profiled in media campaigns? Should the state assume some of the fiscal burdens that result from the tourist industry?

After a period of excessive boosterism, the literature on tourism as an economic development strategy has begun to address the question of its distinct costs: financial, social, and environmental. Too much tourism — for example, more than the capacity of a rural community or region can accommodate — increases the need for public services — especially police and health services — causes congestion, changes land use patterns and produces sprawl development, and alters the nature of the community. This recognition of the costs resulting from tourism and recreational development has led professional planners to coin the term "ecotourism," which seeks to find "the balance between two seemingly conflicting positions: preservation of natural resources and public use of that same environment."[76]

Rural residents in many communities — in New England, Florida, Hawaii, and the Rocky Mountain states, especially — can attest to transformation of their communities from robust tourism and recreation industries. The penalty of unconstrained success from a tourism strategy is that the visitors drawn to picturesque places may go on to consume those communities. Thomas Rawls, author of *Small Places*, observed:

> The newcomers have money and are using it to transform the rural town into a neosuburb — better schools, paved roads, rising real estate values, and property taxes to match. The next generation of natives can't afford to live in their hometowns.[77]

The tourism industry has also been criticized because of its generally low-paying jobs, which cause a social conflict between the less affluent residents who serve and the more affluent visitors who are served. A summary of the literature concluded:

> Many new tourism jobs require little training of rural residents because of the menial nature of the jobs, such as food servers, maids, and retail clerks. These jobs are often seasonal, with low wages, few benefits, and little chance for advancement. The better paying tourism jobs, such as those in management, could require the costly training of rural residents and, as a result, often go to outsiders.[78]

Many rural residents believe that both the financial costs and the social changes resulting from tourism are justified by the benefits derived; others do not. The controversies surrounding tourism as an economic development strategy illustrate the argument made in chapter 3 that development is a political, as well as economic, process. Both the scale and pace of development resulting from tourism may determine its acceptance among rural residents.[79] Another key variable is whether other employment opportunities exist in or near these transforming communities. For example, rural communities with the fewest viable economic options may be the most eager for the benefits from tourism — despite its costs — in much the same way that it is considered better to have a lower-paying job than no job at all.

These criticisms of tourism should not dissuade community leaders from developing tourism strategies as part of a broader effort to diversify their local economies. Nor should these observations discourage state promotion activities and professional media campaigns to market their state's boundless opportunities for sightseeing, recreation, and discovery. State policymakers and rural community leaders should, however, understand that this industry imposes costs along with providing employment and other benefits. In moderation, tourism can provide an important stimulus to rural economies and a prudent use of rural comparative advantages.

Resources for Natural Resources Development

- H. Richard Anderson, Northern Economic Initiatives Corporation, 1009 West Ridge Street, Marquette, Michigan 49855; 906.228.5571.

- "Bucking the System: Lessons from One Foundation's Investments in Agricultural Diversification," William Nothdurft and Mark Popovich, *Northwest Report*, Newsletter of Northwest Area Foundation, St. Paul, Minnesota, April 1991.

- *Communities in the Lead: The Northwest Rural Development Sourcebook* by Harold Fossum, Northwest Policy Center, 327 Parrington Hall, DC-14, Seattle, Washington 98195; 206.543.7900.

- *Going Global: How Europe Helps Small Firms Export*, William E. Nothdurft, the Brookings Institution, Washington, D.C. 20036.

- *Recouple — Natural Resource Strategies for Rural Economic Development*, Midwest Research Institute, 425 Volker Boulevard, Kansas City, Missouri 64110.

- *Renewing America: Natural Resource Assets and State Economic Development* Council of Governors' Policy Advisors, Suite 390, 400 N. Capitol, Washington, D.C. 20001; 202.624.3586.

- *Tourism as a Rural Economic Development Tool: An Exploration of the Literature*, Martha Frederick, Bibliographies and Literature of Agriculture No. 122, Economic Research Service, USDA, Washington, D.C. 20005-4788; Copies available for $8 each by calling 1.800.999.6779.

Collaborative Efforts on Rural Development

Important new initiatives have begun in recent years to foster the coordination and cooperation of many different organizations that share a common interest in the economic viability of rural communities. The most prominent of these was the organization of State Rural Development Councils (SRDC) in most of the states by the Economic Policy Council Working Group on Rural Development. Begun as a pilot program with only eight states in 1990 (Kansas, Maine, Mississippi, Oregon, South Carolina, South Dakota, Texas, and Washington), these SRDCs were organized in twenty-eight additional states by the end of 1992. The organizational objective of this program is to improve resource coordination to assist rural communities through interagency, intergovernmental, and public/private collaboration. These SRDCs were created as a federal-state partnership and generally include the participation of the key agency directors from both state government and federal regional offices, as well as leaders from the private sector and native American tribes.

As any student of government can attest, there are numerous opportunities to improve the allocation of public resources through better communication, cooperation, and coordination. The SRDCs have initially done well on that task. Here are a few examples:

- Applications for small business loans from various state and federal agencies in Kansas were streamlined and modified to create a single application form for all public-sector loan programs;

- In South Carolina, the state council helped six rural communities work together to create a regional water and waste system;

- A small town had received a Community Facility loan of $146,700 from Farmers Home Administration (FmHA), but its leaders were frustrated to learn that the annual audit cost more than $4,500 — almost as much as the annual principal and interest payment. As a result of SRDC advocacy and intervention by federal officials involved in developing this initiative, FmHA was persuaded to waive the annual audit requirement for small communities. USDA officials have estimated that FmHA's decision may save rural communities more than $400 million; and

- Before the council was organized in South Dakota, the controversial issue of the appropriate recreational use of a dam-created lake was in the courts; the council was successful in facilitating a dialogue between the governor's office and the Army Corps of Engineers that may resolve the dispute.[80]

The potential contribution of the SRDCs in achieving rural development objectives rests with their ability to chart independent missions that motivate their participants and sustain a high level of activity and commitment to this new organizational structure. Many of the SRDCs have achieved this high standard; others are still in the early stages of forming an organizational identity and action agenda.[81]

Recent efforts through the Maine SRDC provide a vivid illustration of the potential contribution of this organizational structure and interagency approach. For more than a year, a subcommittee of the SRDC, called the working group on value added, has been meeting to develop a model for disseminating information about new technologies to the state's secondary wood products industry. The participants of this working group, which includes experts from several state and federal agencies, regional, and local development agencies, industry organizations, and the private sector, are convinced that the failure of Maine resource industries to adopt new technologies and explore new markets prevents them from fully developing their value-added potential. Many of the service providers in the secondary wood industry have good access to the latest technologies, but lack the organizational resources to disseminate such information. Meanwhile, other service providers have little information, but have organizational resources with potential for use in disseminating technological information. The working group has a strong commitment to developing implementation strategies for disseminating information and technologies to the secondary wood products industry. The dissemination model could be adapted eventually to serve other resource-based industries in Maine as well as in other states.

Several states began collaborative efforts that preceded the SRDCs and have served as models for them. An NGA study entitled *State-Federal Collaboration on Rural Development* summarized the collaborative efforts of the Idaho Rural Development Council under Governor Andrus' leadership, the Maine Rural Development Committee established by Governor Joseph E. Brennan and expanded by Governor John R. McKernan, Jr., the Oklahoma Rural Enterprise Team, and the Rural Development Coordinating Council created by Wisconsin Governor Tommy Thompson. The report also summarized other collaborative efforts by state and federal agencies in developing medical facilities in Montana, in community development projects in California, Colorado, Illinois, and West

Virginia, in collaboration with the Appalachian Regional Commission, and in providing loans to firms that add value to agricultural products in rural communities in South Dakota.[82]

These efforts and the subsequent development of the SRDCs have provided a regular forum for those committed to rural development issues to exchange information, learn from each other, explore common strategies, and pool resources to achieve common objectives. They also have developed a working network of professionals who care about improving the quality of life in the rural communities of their states. These are important functions; they define, in part, the development capacity of rural organizations to adapt, respond to, and shape changes in the future that will affect rural economies.

Another example comes from Nebraska's approach to involving many organizations from every part of its state in its economic development program. After the election of Governor Nelson in 1990, economic development officials worked closely with the newly created State's Rural Development Commission to create the Nebraska Development Network. Its goal is: *People, communities, and businesses that succeed in a global economy*. The network includes most of the organizations and institutions that promote economic or community development and each of these service providers has signed a memo of understanding with the network. Its members are organized into regional groups to create and support community based capacity. Indeed, the network "is committed to creating and supporting this capacity *in communities* — community by community, groups of communities by groups of communities, region by region." The coordination of the network is performed by the forum, which provides strategic planning, resource allocation, and evaluation.[83]

The concept of industrial or business networks has also been proposed as a strategy to promote rural competitiveness. These networks are simply voluntary arrangements, usually through a voluntary organization, that enable firms to undertake cost-sharing or joint action in critical business operations. Most proponents of this idea refer to the successful industrial networks in Europe, especially those in Denmark and Italy, as a mechanism to assist small and medium-size firms to innovate and compete in global markets. But the model for some of the proposed functions of industrial networks is uniquely American — the agricultural extension program. Stuart Rosenfeld, an expert on industrial networks, made this analogy:

> At the turn of the century, when information was scarce and communication systems unsophisticated, agriculture established county agents (initially called "county farm advisors") to inform and advise farmers about

new technology and best practice. This is still the most popular model for effectively deploying information, but farmers are well-educated in the value of information disseminated by county agents.... Manufacturers are not. Public programs and services are rarely if ever addressed by public education and are unfamiliar to most manufacturers.[84]

Ann Crittenden, the author of a book on national economic policy, observed that the agricultural extension program "has an annual budget of $1.1 billion and a staff of sixteen thousand people (including one extension worker for every 150 or so farmers — for a sector that contributes less than 2 percent to our GDP (Gross Domestic Product)." Crittenden also claimed that the industrial-extension program was adopted in Japan after World War II at the urging of the New Dealers who ran the Occupation. For comparative purposes, Japan now spends an estimated $500 million a year on industrial extension and technology. According to Crittenden, twenty-three states support technology-extension centers, but even the best ones help only a few hundred firms a year.[85] Many advocates have urged Congress to enact a federal industrial extension program.[86]

In contrast to a federal industrial extension program, the notion of creating "industrial networks" has greater appeal to some because technical assistance and business support services would be provided through voluntary organizations, instead of through the traditional model of government as the primary service provider. An organization that receives most of its funding from membership and fees for contracted services clearly has an institutional incentive to provide appropriate and high-quality services. Flexible manufacturing networks might also have distinct organizational advantages in setting quality standards for participating firms or in selectively targeting firms within important sectors of the local or regional economy.

According to Ann Crittenden, "more than 3000 of Denmark's 7300 manufacturing companies were actively involved in networks, cooperating in marketing, the joint use of advanced technology, product development, and quality control." Networks in various stages of development have been established in this country in various industries such as woodworking, metalworking, and forging.[87] Doug Ross has identified networks among auto suppliers in Michigan, heat treaters in Ohio, machine shops in Indiana, and among Florida aerospace suppliers.[88] (See box 4-8 for a brief summary of flexible manufacturing networks in Ohio.)

The state role in assisting industrial networks varies considerably. Oregon has been among the leaders in following the Denmark model, in which public funds are used to finance feasibility studies and provide initial support. Oregon's Economic Development Department "has funded the feasibility studies for a dozen flexible manufacturing networks, has a dozen more proposals in hand, and has budgeted for a hundred more in the coming two years."[89]

The Clinton administration is likely to propose a greater role for the federal government in assisting small and medium-size industrial firms. The 1988 Trade Act established Manufacturing Technology Centers that are administered by the Commerce Department's National Institute for Standards and

---

Box 4-8
Flexible Manufacturing Networks in Ohio

The Appalachian Center for Economic Networks (ACEnet) was founded in 1991 with support from the state of Ohio. Its goal is to create an institutional arrangement that will create relatively high-skill, high-wage jobs for an eleven-county rural area in southern Ohio by enabling local manufacturers to work together to produce marketable goods.

In 1991, ACEnet established a group of flexible manufacturing networks to produce adjustable housing components that can accommodate the special needs of the disabled and elderly. For example, one component produced by one of the networks is a kitchen sink that can be easily adjusted to any height. ACEnet staff identified a market niche that matched the manufacturing capabilities of a collection of small local firms. No single firm had the capability to identify the market, design the products, and manufacture the products. By working with ACEnet, the networks have been able to successfully create, manufacture, and market these special housing components.

ACEnet staff and network participants expect that network membership will evolve over time.... Thus, the word "flexible" is an extremely accurate description of the manufacturing networks that are being created in southern Ohio.

Source: David W. Sears, John M. Redman, Richard L. Gardner, and Stephen J. Adams, *Gearing Up for Success: Organizing a State for Rural Development* (Washington, D.C.: The Aspen Institute, 1992), 30. See also ACEnet. "FMN Project Poised to Begin Production," Network News 3, no.1 (November 1991): 2.

Technology. During the 1992 presidential campaign, candidate Clinton proposed establishing as many as 170 manufacturing extension centers throughout the nation to assist small firms in becoming more competitive. He also proposed that the Defense Advanced Research Project Agency (DARPA), an agency funded in the military budget, expand its focus to assist commercial as well as military research and development projects. In addition, Rosenfeld has observed that as governor, Bill Clinton traveled to Emilia-Romagna "to witness firsthand the success of small and medium-size manufacturing enterprises (SMEs) in Third Italy" and in 1983 created the Arkansas Science and Technology Authority to manage a new approach to economic development, which included "a challenge grant program for promising pilot networks of small and medium-size manufacturers." [90]

One of the myths about rural America is that manufacturing is unimportant or nonexistent. Manufacturing provides approximately 17 percent of the employment in nonmetropolitan counties, which is roughly the same as that of the nation. Almost one-third of the nonmetropolitan population lives in manufacturing-dependent counties, which are defined as receiving at least 30 percent of their income from that sector. Moreover, many of these jobs are in routine production, which faces very tough global competition. Both the workers and their communities face the growing threat that those firms will relocate to lower wage, industrializing nations. *Efforts to assist domestic small and medium-size manufacturing firms to innovate, apply advanced technologies, and become more competitive should be important components in virtually every state's rural development policy.*

Resources for Collaborative Efforts

- Appalachian Center for Economic Networks (ACENET), 94 North Columbus Road, Athens, Ohio 45701; 614.592.3854.

- Stephen Buttress, Director of Economic Development, Box 94666, Lincoln, Neb. 68509-4666; 402.471.3747.

- *A Catalogue of U.S. Manufacturing Networks* by Gregg A. Lichtenstein, State Technology Extension Program. NIST, Building 221, Room A343, Gaithersburg, Md. 20899; 301.975.3086.

- Joseph Cortright, Executive Officer, Joint Legislative Committee on Trade and Economic Development, State Capitol, Room 132, Salem, Oreg. 97310; 503.378.8811.

- *The Entrepreneurial Economy Review* vol.9 no.1 (Spring 1991) Corporation for Enterprise Development, 777 North Capitol, Washington, D.C. 20001; 202.408.9788; Also contact: Robert Friedman in West Coast office: 415.495.2333.

- *Entrepreneurial Strategies: Readings on Flexible Manufacturing Networks*, Northwest Policy Center, University of Washington, 327 Parrington Hall, DC-14, Seattle, Wash. 98195; 206.543.7900.

- *An Introductory Guide: Flexible Business Networks* (includes excellent bibliography), German Marshall Fund of the United States (GMF), 11 Dupont Circle, N.W., Washington, D.C. 20036; 202.745.3950.

- The Modernization Forum, 20501 Ford Road, Suite 200, Dearborn, Mich. 48128; 313.271.2791.

- National Institute of Standards and Technology (NIST), State Technology Extension Program, Building 221, Room A343, Gaithersburg, Md. 20899; 301.975.3086.

- Stuart Rosenfeld, Regional Technology Strategies, Inc. (RTS), 218 Vance Street, Chapel Hill, N.C. 27516; 919.933.6699.

- National Initiative on Rural America, USDA, 14th and Independence, S.W., Washington, D.C. 20250.

- *Smart Firms in Small Towns*, Stuart Rosenfeld with Philip Shapira and J. Trent Williams, The Aspen Institute, 1333 New Hampshire Ave. N.W., Suite 1070, Washington, D.C. 20036.

- *State-Federal Collaboration on Rural Development*, Thomas Unruh and Jay Kayne, National Governors' Association, 444 North Capitol St., Washington, D.C. 20001-1572.

Community Leadership and Capacity Building

Local economic development activities are often considered to be a subset of broader community development objectives. This is an eminently logical perspective for the majority of communities that have stable, vibrant economies. For much of rural America, however, the mission of generating employment and income to maintain viable local economies supersedes all other community objectives. Those communities capable of nurturing local leadership and development capacity sufficient to achieve their primary economic development objectives will often also generate the resources, leadership, and organizational capacity to address other community problems.

Effective community leadership occurs when chronic problems are well understood and an organized response is planned and implemented that diminishes the severity of these problems in the future. Some of the best insights about community leadership come from organizations that have assisted struggling rural communities. The Rural Initiatives Program of Pioneer hi-Bred International, Inc., a seed company located in Des Moines, Iowa, has assisted many farm-dependent communities in strengthening their leadership skills. The Heartland Center for Leadership Development in Lincoln, Nebraska, began similar work in the field by observing closely the key characteristics of successful communities: see box 4-9 for the Heartland Center's "Twenty Clues to Rural Community Survival." Many public utilities, such as the Southwestern Public Service Company, have been active in assisting rural communities to develop leadership skills, assess their strengths and weaknesses, and initiate economic development strategies. The cooperative extension program in many states has been a leader in this task. The Ford and Kellogg foundations have also generously supported rural leadership development and community assessment programs.

Designing Development Strategies in Small Towns by Glen Pulver and David Dodson, another helpful publication in the Aspen Institute's Best Practices Series, presented several models for providing community assessment assistance: the continuous local assistance model, the regional resource model, the parachute model, and the leadership training model. Approaches such as these are likely to vary among the states. This is the way they articulated the rationale for state involvement in community assessment programs:

> Few rural towns or counties have a sufficient combination of institutional capacity, financial resources, leadership depth, and direct access to specialized knowledge to be able to undertake rigorous, independent assessment.... Yet it should be clear that states also benefit when localities are able to clarify their most urgent needs, catalogue their resources, and analyze how they can improve their standing. Not only may self-scrutiny lead to more intelligent use of state programs, but it invariably unleashes local resources. The net result is often much stronger rural economies, higher living standards, and a healthier state fiscal base.[91]

This book also summarized how several states supported community assessment: in Wisconsin, the cooperative extension program has assumed this responsibility; in South Carolina, the Local Economic Action Planning program works

Box 4-9
Twenty Clues to Rural Community Survival

1. Evidence of community pride.

2. Emphasis on quality in business and community life.

3. Willingness to invest in the future.

4. Participatory approach to community decision-making.

5. Cooperative community spirit.

6. Realistic appraisal of future opportunities.

7. Awareness of competitive positioning.

8. Knowledge of the physical environment.

9. Active economic development program.

10. Deliberate transition of power to a younger generation of leaders.

11. Acceptance of women in leadership roles.

12. Strong belief in and support for education.

13. Problem-solving approach to providing health care.

14. Strong multi-generational family orientation.

15. Strong presence of traditional institutions that are integral to community life.

16. Attention to sound and well-maintained infrastructure.

17. Careful use of fiscal resources.

18. Sophisticated use of information resources.

19. Willingness to seek help from the outside.

20. Conviction that, in the long run, you have to do it yourself.

Source: Heartland Center for Leadership Development, (1987), 941 O Street, Suite 920, Lincoln, Nebraska 68508; 402.474.7667.

with the state's 34 nonmetropolitan counties; and in Oregon, the Rural Development Initiative, Inc. has been established to help "Oregon's rural communities generate realistic options for their economic future by building their capacity to plan and act strategically." [92] Another approach was taken in Washington State when it created a network of local development agencies throughout the state; this network was intended to provide professional assistance to communities and to build local capacity for development. The state allocated more than $4 million during 1990-1991 for these development agencies.[93]

Fiscally challenged state governments are likely to be cautious about assuming greater responsibility in providing community assessment assistance or the resources with which communities can develop local capacities for development. States clearly do not have sufficient resources to satisfy every need identified by every community. The Gem Communities program in Idaho represents a selective, targeted mechanism for assisting those communities willing to meet the threshold of organizational commitment and collective concern about their economic future. Under this program, a city, county, or group of counties apply to become a Gem Community. The application and review process helps community leaders assess and articulate their community's objectives. Selected communities are then given assistance from the state Department of Commerce. Requiring the demonstration of community self-help activities is often used by state governments as a rationing or targeting device for directing scarce state resources.

Another promising approach is state funding for regional economic development activities and strategies. Theoretically, this could encourage individual entities — towns, counties, and cities — to cooperate more on regional economic development efforts (and on other mutual problems); it could diminish the short-sighted, parochial focus that often dominates small town rivalries; it could even yield a collective recognition that the region itself represents the logical economic unit and is one that projects a common identity. These were among the considerations that led to the Oregon Regional Strategies Program in 1987. This program recognized and supported the development efforts of fifteen regions throughout the state, and assisted each of them in developing regional economic development strategies and specific projects. An evaluation of this program called it "ground breaking — no other state has enacted a regional or rural development program of this scope or magnitude." [94]

Community leaders who have learned to cooperate rather than compete also provide important lessons. *The New York Times* profiled some of the successful strategies developed by Nestbuilders Network, which meets monthly to plot the survival of Custer County:

At the end of each meeting, they have what they call a "wild and crazy" session to brainstorm for new ideas. There are two rules: No one can laugh at an idea, and no one can say,"That won't work here."

As one session, they tried to figure out a way to bring tourists to this remote stretch of Nebraska. But what did the countryside have to offer?

"There is plenty of wind," said someone, half in jest.

"That's it," someone else replied. "Everyone liked to fly kites as a kid. We'll have a kite-flying festival."

The celebration drew visitors from seven states, and the stores and restaurants of the county profited.[95]

Resources for Community Leadership and Capacity Building

- *Creating an Economic Development Action Plan: A Guide for Development Professionals*, Thomas S. Lyons and Roger E. Hamlin, New York: Praeger, 1991.

- *Community Development Training Manual*, ed., Cheryl Pink and Noreen Scott, Laura Adams Dudley, (1990) Southwestern Public Service Company and State of New Mexico; Southwestern Public Service Company, Economic Development Department, P.O.Box 1261, Amarillo, Texas 79170.

- *Designing Development Strategies in Small Towns*, Glen Pulver and David Dodson, The Aspen Institute, 1333 New Hampshire Ave.N.W., Suite 1070, Washington, D.C. 20036.

- *Economic Development for Small Communities and Rural Areas*, Phillip D. Phillips, Community Information and Education Service Programs, Office of Continuing Education and Public Service, University of Illinois at Urbana-Champaign, Illinois, 1990.

- "The New Localism: You Can't Wring Your Hands and Roll Up Your Sleeves at the Same Time." William Schweke and Graham S. Toft, *Entrepreneurial Economy Review* (Winter 1991): 3-8, Corporation for Enterprise Development, 777 North Capitol, Washington, D.C. 20002; 202.745.3950.

- *Harvesting Hometown Jobs*, Nancy T. Stark, National Association of Towns and Townships, 1522 K St., N.W., Suite 730, Washington, D.C. 20005; 202.737.5200.

- Michael Kinsley, Economic Renewal Program, Rocky Mountain Institute, 1739 Snowmass Creek Road, Snowmass, Colorado 81654-9199.

- *Taking Charge: Economic Development in Small Communities*, North Central Regional Center for Rural Development, Iowa State University, Ames, Iowa 50011.

• *Utilities and Industries: New Partnerships for Rural Development* by Charles Bartsch and Diane De Vaul, The Northeast-Midwest Institute, Available from The Aspen Institute, 1333 New Hampshire Avenue, N. W., Suite 1070, Washington, D.C. 20036; 202.736.5804.

Public Infrastructure

Although telecommunications systems, in theory, can substantially reduce the traditional rural disadvantages of isolation and the distance penalty, other systems are also important to facilitating economic development. As discussed, the canals, railroads, and highways of the nineteenth century were essential to link rural areas with urban markets. This physical linkage remains very important for rural economies, which is the reason that both highways and airports are often viewed as strategic infrastructure investments for rural development.[96]

Infrastructure has been defined as "the permanent physical installations and facilities supporting socioeconomic activities in a community, region or nation." [97] The term includes telephone systems, highways, airports, schools, hospitals, water treatment facilities, fire stations, parks and recreation facilities, libraries, museums, and cultural facilities.

The conventional approach has been to advocate for public infrastructure investments that lie within a narrowly defined category such as highways, airports, and telecommunication systems, as a means to induce the economic development of a community, region, or state. A report by the Economic Research Service, *Infrastructure Investment and Economic Development*, identified four ways in which infrastructure investment could stimulate economic development in a rural region:

• To improve efficiency or enable business expansion (i.e., "Opening a new four-lane highway from the community to a nearby Interstate highway may reduce the distance (time) to the closest metro areas; this investment might be expected to promote development by improving efficiency through reduced transportation costs and shipping times.");

• To provide short-term stimulus through construction jobs;

• To improve the attractiveness of a community as a place to live and work; and

• To boost the community morale, which might encourage other investments.[98]

These rationales for infrastructure investment are difficult to assess. The first one expresses the rationale for public intervention to achieve greater efficiency, as mentioned in chapter 2, which is persuasive, though often difficult to measure. How would one measure the efficiency gains or economic benefits from the new highway? The second argument is specious because the short-term stimulus has little, if any, long-term impact on a region's economic growth or development. The third argument is quite important, but also difficult to measure. And the last argument is impossible to quantify.

These difficulties have led economists into the social science maze of causality: does public infrastructure investment stimulate economic growth, or does a higher level of economic growth increase the demand for additional infrastructure investment? One economist, for example, thought that if public investment preceded private, "then local areas could use public funds for infrastructure development to achieve growth," but he found instead that "causation ran in both directions, depending on location and time." [99] It is for these reasons that most economists prefer the conclusion that infrastructure, like education, is generally a *necessary, but not always sufficient condition to stimulate economic development.*

Does maintaining a high quality of life serve important economic development objectives? What are the other facilities and public services that make a community attractive both to investors and to workers? Business and people have become very mobile in our society. Both have moved and will continue to move to other, more desirable locations to satisfy their needs. Achieving the quality of life desired by a community, by maintaining adequate public infrastructure systems and facilities, is essential to the long-term economic viability of the community. In *Job Creation in America*, David Birch identified five criteria that "are especially important to innovative, entrepreneurial firms: educational resources, particularly higher education; quality of labor; quality of government; telecommunications; and quality of life."[100]

Economic development cannot thrive nor be sustained in a social environment that fails to meet the quality-of-life expectations of the community. The advanced technologies of today and tomorrow may grant such mobility to both firms and workers that their locational decisions could largely rest upon their preferred quality-of-life choices. Indeed, if this trend continues, those rural communities with quality public facilities, services, and amenities may well have distinct comparative advantages for future employment growth.

Planning public infrastructure investments as a rural development strategy is a laudable challenge and may be one for which state governments should assume primary responsibility. As discussed in chapter 2, one of rural America's economic disadvantages is its diminished fiscal capacity. State governments, therefore, should devote special attention to both the immediate and longer-term infrastructure needs of its rural communities. Perhaps one of the strongest rationales for state funding is that they will increase regional economic efficiency; (theoretically, the new highway could improve the efficiency of both the rural and urban economies). Indeed, with so many competing demands and such scarce capital funds, state governments should plan strategically for infrastructure projects in rural communities. Public investments to improve regional airports or major trade centers might be considered important strategic priorities.

State governments, however, also have equity concerns about the distribution of essential public services, especially those that provide health and safety benefits such as water and sewer facilities. Too much emphasis on the economic development rationale could shift state capital expenditures away from equally valuable infrastructure projects that provide essential services and enhance the richness of community life.

Considering the fiscal distress of rural town and county governments, state governments should reevaluate whether their expertise in planning, facilitating, coordinating, and capital budgeting is appropriately directed in assisting rural communities with their public infrastructure needs. Several years ago, states interested in encouraging school districts to improve their facilities provided matching grants for new construction and major rehabilitation of existing buildings. Perhaps following this current era of fiscal constraints in the public sector, similar capital expenditure programs, specifically designed to aid rural communities, will be enacted. In the interim, however, state governments could prepare multiyear, regional capital budgets for public infrastructure projects that reflect both the efficiency and equity concerns of state government. Taxpayers and voters might well appreciate additional information about future state capital expenditures planned for their communities and regions.

Resources for Public Infrastructure Strategies

- *Infrastructure Investment and Economic Development: Rural Strategies for the 1990s*, USDA, Economic Research Service, 1303 New York Avenue NW, Washington, D.C. 20005-4788. Copies available for $11 each: 1.800.999.6779 or write to: ERS-NASS, P.O.Box 1608, Rockville, Md. 20849-1608.

- *The Wealth of States: Policies for a Dynamic Economy*, Chapter 7: "Investing In Public Capital," by Roger Vaughan, Robert Pollard, and Barbara Dyer. CGPA, Suite 390, 400 North Capitol Street, Washington, D.C. 20001.

Notes:

1. Gerald M. Meier and Dudley Seers, eds., *Pioneers in Development* (New York: Oxford University Press for the World Bank, 1984), 219-220; as quoted in W.W. Rostow, *Theorists of Economic Growth from David Hume to the Present* (New York: Oxford University Press, 1990), 411.

2. Ibid., 397-398.

3. The "uncoupled" phrase and concept comes from Peter F. Drucker, "The Changed World Economy," *Foreign Affairs*, (New York: Council on Foreign Relations, Spring 1986). Drucker has been emphatic in his assessment of the current economic transformation. In *Post-Capitalist Society* (New York: HarperCollins, 1993), 8, Drucker wrote:

> The basic economic resource—"the means of production," to use the economist's term—is no longer capital, nor natural resources (the economist's land), nor "labor." *It is and will be knowledge.* The central wealth-creating activities will be neither the allocation of capital to productive uses, nor "labor"—the two poles of nineteenth- and twentieth-century economic theory, whether classical, Marxist, Keynesian, or neo-classical. Value is now created by "productivity" and "innovation," both applications of knowledge to work.... The economic challenge of the post-capitalist society will therefore be the productivity of knowledge work and the knowledge worker.

Also see Rostow, *Theorists of Economic Growth*.

4. As quoted in Roger Vaughan, Robert Pollard, and Barbara Dyer, *The Wealth of States: Policies for a Dynamic Economy* (Washington, D.C.: CSPA, 1985), 98. See also W.W. Rostow, *Theorists of Economic Growth*—in Rostow's treatment of Alfred Marshall (p.169), he wrote: "Clearly, Marshall regarded increased outlays for education in England of his day as a form of investment subject to increasing returns. His analysis—and its predecessor analyses back to Hume and Adam Smith—makes it difficult to regard the emergence of investment in "human capital" in post-1945 development economics as a pioneering revelation."

Indeed, here is Marshall in *Principles of Economics*, 8th ed. (London: Macmillan, 1930), 212, as quoted by Rostow:

> There is no extravagance more prejudicial to the growth of national wealth than that wasteful negligence which allows genius that happens to be born of lowly parentage to expend itself in lowly work. No change would conduce so much to a rapid increase of material wealth as an improvement in our schools, and especially those of the middle grades, provided it be combined with an extensive system of scholarships, which will enable the clever son of a working man to rise gradually from school to school till he has the best theoretical and practical education which the age can give.

Rostow quoted J.M. Clark, who wrote in 1923: "Knowledge is the only instrument of production not subject to diminishing returns." (p. 462), and he quoted Jacob Vinter, who wrote in 1953: "The first requirements for the high labour productivity under modern conditions are that the masses of the population shall be literate, healthy, and sufficiently well fed to be strong and energetic." (p.382).

5. Peter F. Drucker, *People and Performance: The Best of Peter Drucker on Management* (New York: Harper & Row, 1977), 94.

6. *America's Choice: high skills or low wages*, Report of the Commission on the Skills of the American Workforce, (Rochester, New York: National Center on Education and the Economy, June, 1990), 1-9.

7. *Wall Street Journal*, Special Section on Education, February 9, 1990, as quoted in David A. McGranahan, "Introduction," *Education and Rural Economic Development: Rural Strategies for the 1990's*, ed., Richard W. Long (Washington, D.C.: Economic Research Service, U.S. Department of Agriculture, September 1991), 1.

8. Anthony Patrick Carnevale, *America and the New Economy*. (Alexandria, Va.: The American Society for Training and Development, U.S. Dept. of Labor 1991), 1-2.

9. J. Norman Reid, "The Context of Rural Education: The Economy and Population of Rural America," *The Condition of Education in Rural Schools*, (Washington, D.C.: U.S. Department of Education, Office of Educational Research and Improvement, forthcoming), chapter II, p.7.

10. Richard W. Long, ed., *Education and Rural Economic Development*, 1. This is from the abstract:

> The 1980s found the U.S. economy vulnerable in the global marketplace. Many observers have argued that workforce education and skill levels are too low. Rural workers have especially low levels of education and the 1980s were especially unkind to these workers.... *The central conclusion is that education's potential as a local area rural development strategy is probably quite limited*, but that the need to raise education and training levels for rural youth, whenever they will work, is critical. (Emphasis added.)

11. Ibid., 7.

12. David A. McGranahan, "Introduction," *Education and Rural Economic Development*, 1-11.

13. Paul L. Swaim and Ruy A. Teixeira, "Education and Training Policy: Skill Upgrading Options for the Rural Workforce," *Education and Rural Economic Development*, 156.

14. McGranahan, "Introduction," 10.

15. Joyce D. Stern, ed., *The Condition of Education in Rural Schools*, Office of Educational Research and Improvement (OERI), (Washington, D.C.: U.S. Department of Education, forthcoming), chapter 8.

16. Ibid., 7-8.

17. Ibid., chapter 7, p.8.

18. Ibid., 7.

19. Doug Ross, "Enterprise Economics on the Front Line: Empowering Firms and Workers to Win," in *Mandate for Change*, ed., Will Marshall and Martin Schram (New York: Berkley Progressive Policy Institute, 1993), 70-71.

20. Peter T. Kilborn, "Innovative Program in California Aids Those With Outdated Skills," *New York Times*, 27 November 1992, p. D-7.

21. Browne et al., *Sacred Cows and Hot Potatoes: Agrarian Myths in Agricultural Policy* (Boulder, Colo.: Westview Press, 1992), 26.

22. Governor Robert Kerrey, "Foreword," *The Challenge of Telecommunications: State Regulatory and Tax Policies*, ed. Barbara Dyer, Draft 8/86 (Washington, D.C.: CSPA, 1986).

23. U.S. Congress, Office of Technology Assessment, *Rural America at the Crossroads: Networking for the Future*, OTA TCT-471 (Washington, D.C.: U.S. Government Printing Office, April 1991), 66-67.

24. Steven Prokesch, "Wiring Into the Future: The High Stakes of Telecommunications," *New York Times*, 12 January 1993, p. B1.

25. For a good summary on this topic, see Nancy Ginn Helme, *New Alliances in Innovation: A Guide to Encouraging Innovative Applications of New Communication Technologies to Address State Problems*, (Washington, D.C.: Council of Governors' Policy Advisors, 1992), 32.

26. Edwin B. Parker and Heather E. Hudson with Don A. Dillman, Sharon Strover, and Fredrick Williams, *Electronic Byways: State Policies for Rural Development Through Telecommunications* (Boulder, Colo.: Westview Press/Aspen Institute, 1992), 3.

27. Ibid., 16-17.

28. Personal communication from Edwin B. Parker, President of Parker Telecommunications, Gleneden, Oregon.

29. *Economic Development Abroad* 5, no.3, (Washington, D.C.: National Council for Urban Economic Development and the Academy for State and Local Government, February 1991).

30. Brian O'Reilly, 1992, "Your New Global Work Force," *Fortune* 126, no.13, (December 14, 1992): 56.

31. Helme, *New Alliances*, 34.

32. Ibid.

33. *Nebraska Development Network Digest* 1, no. 2, Nebraska Development Network Office (Lincoln, Nebr.: Nebraska Development Network, Fall, 1992): 9.

34. See OTA, *Rural America at the Crossroads*, 28.

35. Alan M. Webber, "What's So New About the New Economy?" *Harvard Business Review* (January-February 1993): 25; Lest there is any doubt about the acceleration of advanced technologies and the potential impact that they will have upon rural America, note this report from Japan by Andrew Pollack in the *New York Times* ("Computer Translator Phones to Try to Compensate for Babel," 29 January 1993):

> Toshiyuki Takazawa sat down at a bank of powerful computers here this afternoon and spoke into a microphone, "Moshimoshi," he said.
> Instantly, the computers whirred to life, furiously digesting and analyzing this morsel of Japanese speech. Twelve seconds later and half a world away, a computer in Pittsburgh spoke, conveying Dr. Takazawa's message in English. "Hello," it said, in its electronic voice.

36. Peter F. Drucker, *Innovation and Entrepreneurship: Practice and Principles*, (New York: Harper and Row, 1985), 21.

37. Ibid., 7.

38. Vaughan et al., *The Wealth of States*, 59. Also see chapter 4, "The Entrepreneurial Environment," generally.

39. Ibid., 57.

40. Everett M. Rogers and Judith K. Larsen, *Silicon Valley Fever: Growth of High-Technology Culture* (New York: Basic Books, 1984), 234; as quoted in Vaughan et al., Wealth of States, 56.

41. Mark G. Popovich, *New Business, Entrepreneurship and Rural Development: State Policies and Generating Rural Growth from Within*, Final Project Report to the Ford Foundation, (Washington, D.C.: Council of Governors' Policy Advisors, 1993), 1.

42. Ibid., 8-13.

43. Ibid., 18-28.

44. Terry F. Buss and Roger J. Vaughan, *On the Rebound: Helping Workers Cope with Plant Closings* (Washington, D.C.: CSPA, 1988), 69.

45. David Osborne, *Laboratories of Democracy* (Boston: Harvard Business School Press, 1988), 34.

46. William E. Nothdurft, "Rural Development Strategies for the 80's " (Presentation to National Association of State Development Agencies, Lexington, Kentucky, December 1, 1986); 3.

47. Richard P. Taub, *Community Capitalism: Banking Strategies and Economic Development* (Boston: Harvard Business School Press, 1988).

48. Patrick J. Sullivan, "Financial Market Intervention as a Rural Development Strategy: An Overview," *Financial Market Intervention as a Rural Development Strategy*, ed. Richard W. Long, ERS Staff Report No.AGES 9070 (Washington, D.C.: Economic Research Service, USDA, December 1990), 1.

49. "Summary," *Financial Market Intervention as a Rural Development Strategy*, ERS Staff Report No. AGES 9070, (Washington, D.C.: Economic Research Service, USDA, December 1990), vi-vii.

50. Frank Maguire, Senior Deputy Comptroller for Legislative and Public Affairs, "Introduction" in *Building Healthy Communities Through Bank Small Business Financing* (Washington, D.C.: Comptroller of the Currency, December 1992). See also in this volume the "Keynote Address," by Stephen R. Steinbrink, Acting Comptroller of the Currency, p. 4, who noted that Section 122 of the FDIC Improvement Act of 1991 "requires the federal regulators to amend the call report to include information on loans to small business and small farms.... Congress wants this information for a reason. Members of Congress are hearing the same stories that I referred to earlier: that banks have stopped making loans to small businesses. So they are taking the first step, gathering information."

51. Ibid., vi.

52. The federal role in financial market intervention to achieve social objectives and minimize market imperfections is beyond the scope of this work. Note, however, that the Community Reinvestment Act of 1977 was intended to halt the common practice of "redlining," which is the arbitrary geographic discrimination in the granting of credit. In addition, the Financial Institutions Reform, Recovery, and Enforcement Act of 1989 has required public disclosure of the ratings of depository institutions' performance in serving their communities. (See below Parzen and Kieschnick, 11-13).

53. Julia Ann Parzen and Michael Hall Kieschnick, *Credit Where It's Due: Development Banking for Communities*, (Philadelphia, Pa.: Temple University Press, 1992), 11.

54. Deborah Markley with Katharine McKee, *Business Finance as a Tool for Development* (Washington, D.C.: The Aspen Institute, 1992), 27.

55. Ibid., 28.

56. Ibid., 20-21.

57. David Osborne, *State Technology Programs: A Preliminary Analysis of Lessons Learned* (Washington, D.C.: CSPA, November 1989), 27-28. Osborne is not alone in this view. Consider this indictment by Parzen and Kieschnick, *Credit Where It's Due*, 13-14:

> Most federal and state loan programs have not been effective development vehicles. Many have lacked lending expertise, which usually must be found outside of public bureaucracies. Some have not been allowed by politicians to take an objective view of investment decisions. A few have been very good programs, but were changed or dismantled at the whim of new public administrations. Because public financial institutions have suffered from such handicaps, business-development lending within the public sector has generally failed regardless of how it is evaluated. This is true of the Small Business Administration, the Economic Development Administration, the Export-Import Bank, and a long list of other public attempts at development finance. Only in the rarest of circumstances should purely public development banks, at any level of government, be attempted.

58. Markley with McKee, *Business Finance*, 27-61; especially see pp. 59-60 for more information about the Northern Economic Initiatives Center.

59. Parzen and Kieschnick, *Credit Where It's Due*, 15-16.

60. Ibid. For more information on the Southern Development Bancorporation, see Markley with McKee, *Business Finance*, 48-49.

61. Jaqueline Novogratz, *Hopeful Change: The Potential of Micro-enterprise Programs as a Community Revitalization Intervention* (New York: The Rockefeller Foundation, 1992), 5.

62. Shorebank Advisory Service, Inc. *Widening the Window of Opportunity: Strategies for the Evolution of Microenterprise Loan Funds*, (Flint, Mich.: Charles Stuart Mott Foundation, 1992), 1.

63. Ibid., 5.

64. Kenneth J. Cooper, "Business Grants, 'Microloans' For Anti-Poverty Program Set," *Washington Post*, 5 June 1992, p. A29.

65. National Association of Development Organizations, "EDA Revolving Loan Fund Survey by NADO Research Foundation," *Economic Development Digest* 2, no. 4, (April 1993), 5.

66. Special Rural Development Finance Issue, *Economic Development Digest* 2, no.4, (April 1993), 1.

67. William E. Nothdurft, *Renewing America: Natural Resource Assets and State Economic Development* (Washington, D.C.: CSPA, 1984), 165.

68. Ibid., 179.

69. Mark G. Popovich, "State Strategies for Promoting Agricultural Exports," in *The Role of State Government in Agriculture*, ed. Enrique Ospina and Cami S. Sims (Morrilton, Ark.: Winrock International Institute for Agricultural Development, 1988), 99.

70. Personal communication from Richard Gardner.

71. Nothdurft, *Renewing America*, 145.

72. Joseph Cortright, *Third Wave Economic Development in Oregon* (Salem, Oreg.: Oregon Joint Legislative Committee on Trade and Economic Development, December 1991), 4-5.

73. *Recouple—Natural Resource Strategies for Rural Economic Development*, Margaret G. Thomas, Project Leader, (Kansas City, Mo.: Midwest Research Institute, 1990), ix.

74. Ibid., x; see also Kirk Johnson, "Environmentalism and the Challenge of Sustainable Development," *The Changing Northwest* (Seattle, Wash.: Northwest Policy Center, June-July 1991).

75. Economic Research Associates, the University of Missouri, and the United States Travel Data Center, *National Policy Study on Rural Tourism and Small Business Development*, (Washington, D.C.: U.S. Department of Commerce, U.S. Travel and Tourism Administration, 1989).

76. Michael C. Brown, "Planning for Ecotourism," *Environment & Development* (Chicago, Ill.: American Planning Association, April 1993). Brown also quoted Peter Murphy's *Tourism: a Community Approach* (New York: Routledge, 1985): "Tourism as a nonconsumptive activity is a fallacy...tourism can lead to the physical deterioration of a landscape if it exceeds the carrying capacity of a destination and is not properly managed."

77. Thomas Rawls, *Small Places*, (Boston: Little, Brown, 1990), Introduction, as quoted in "Saving America's Small Towns," *Utne Reader*, (November-December 1991), 20.

78. Martha Frederick, *Tourism as a Rural Economic Development Tool: As Exploration of the Literature* (Washington, D.C.: U.S. Department of Agriculture, Economic Research Service, 1992), 1.

79. To cite a cross-cultural example, several years ago France began to persuade rural property owners to improve buildings, which had previously sheltered agricultural workers, to rent to foreign visitors. The government provided a financial subsidy for these improvements, required that quality standards be met, and listed the property for the owners. This program, apparently, met its limited objectives: buildings were improved, the owners received the rental income, and the local and national economies benefited from the tourist expenditures. Political controversy and opposition, however, could have been expected if the French land had been sold to foreign newcomers, or if the influx of tourists had changed the fundamental nature of the French rural communities.

80. David W. Sears, John M. Redman, Richard L. Gardner, and Stephen J. Adams, *Gearing Up for Success: Organizing a State for Rural Development* (Washington, D.C.: The Aspen Institute, 1992), 17.

81. For an assessment of the initial development of the SRDCs, see Beryl A. Radin, "Rural Development Councils: An Intergovernmental Coordination Experiment," Publius: *The Journal of Federalism* 22 (Summer 1992): 111-127.

82. Thomas Unruh and Jay Kayne, *State-Federal Collaboration on Rural Development*, Economic Development and Commerce Policy Studies, Center for Policy Research, (Washington, D.C.: National Governors' Association, 1992).

83. Organizational chart, Nebraska Development Network, P.O.Box 94666, Lincoln, Nebraska 68509-4666; 402.471.3805.

84. Stuart A. Rosenfeld, *Competitive Manufacturing: New Strategies for Regional Development* (New Brunswick, N.J.: Center for Urban Policy Research/Rutgers, 1992), 315.

85. Ann Crittenden, *Killing the Sacred Cows: Bold Ideas for a New Economy* (New York: Penguin Books, 1992), 136-141.

86. See Doug Ross, "Enterprise Economics on the Front Lines: Empowering Firms and Workers to Win," *Mandate for Change*, ed. Will Marshall and Martin Schram (New York: Berkley Book/Progressive Policy Institute, 1993), 76-80.

87. Crittenden, *Killing the Sacred Cows*, 140.

88. Ross, "Enterprise Economics," 77.

89. Personal communication from Joseph Cortright, Executive Officer of the Joint Legislative Committee on Trade and Economic Development, State Capitol, Room 132, Salem, Oregon 97310.

90. Rosenfeld, *Competitive Manufacturing*, 310.

91. Glen Pulver and David Dodson, *Designing Development Strategies in Small Towns* (Washington, D.C.: The Aspen Institute, 1992), 11-12.

92. Ibid., 45.

93. David W. Sears et al., *Gearing Up for Success*, 34.

94. Brandon Roberts and Associates & Mt. Auburn Associates, *Oregon Regional Strategies Program Evaluation*, Volume One: Study Findings and Recommendations, (Salem, Oreg.: Oregon Economic Development Department, 1993), 1.

95. Dirk Johnson, "Small Towns Team Up to Fight Bleak Futures," *New York Times*, 1 August 1992, p.1.

96. On the importance of regional airports to economic development, see Michael D. Irwin and John D. Kasarda, "Air Passenger Linkages and Employment Growth in U.S. Metropolitan Areas," *American Sociological Review* 56, (August 1991): 524-537. Note that frequent personal client contact may be important in the development of producer services. Here is a brief excerpt (p.524):

> Activities locate (or differentially survive) in central places because access improves firm efficiency and expands markets, thus making firms more competitive. Accessibility is not fixed, however. It changes constantly as new transportation technologies reshape the spatial economy....
>
> Our working thesis is that the rise of air transportation between 1950 and 1980 substantially reduced frictional constraints to long-distance economic interaction, thereby creating new locational advantages for metropolitan areas. These shifts in locational advantage should be reflected in differential metropolitan-area employment growth rates over this period.
>
> While the rise of the airline network influenced growth potentials in all industries, such changes in air transportation should affect the locational advantages of two industries in particular: manufacturing and producer services (industries providing service to manufacturing and businesses). For both types of industries, the geographic diffusion of production and markets has increased the importance of economic interaction and organizational contact

across space. As manufacturing production sites dispersed, accessibility has become increasingly important for coordination, while for producer services the expansion of the airline network substantially increased the geographic scope of their markets, which rely heavily on nonroutine face-to-face interaction.

97. James Hite, "Financing Infrastructure in Rural America" (Paper presented at the Infrastructure and Rural Economic Development Symposium, Southern Agricultural Economics Association, Nashville, Tennessee, February 8, 1989); as quoted in David W. Sears, Thomas D. Rowley, and J. Norman Reid, "Infrastructure Investment and Economic Development: An Overview," *Infrastructure Investment and Economic Development: Rural Strategies for the 1990's* (Washington, D.C.: USDA, Economic Research Service, December 1990), 1.

98. Sears et al., *Gearing Up for Success*, 4-6.

99. Dewitt John, Sandra S. Batie, and Kim Norris, *A Brighter Future for Rural America? Strategies for Communities and States* (Washington, D.C.: National Governors' Association, 1988), 86; quoting the work of Randall W. Eberts.

100. David Birch, *Job Creation in America: How Our Smallest Companies Put the Most People to Work* (New York: The Free Press, 1987), 140.

The CGPA Process for Setting Priorities

Arnold Toynbee once described the rise and fall of nations in terms of challenge and response. A young nation, he said, is confronted with a challenge for which it finds a successful response. It then grows and prospers. But as time passes, the nature of the challenge changes. And if a nation continues to make the same, once-successful response to the new challenge, it inevitably suffers a decline and eventual failure. As we begin the last two decades of the 20th century, the United States faces such a challenge.   — William S. Anderson, Chairman, NCR Corporation[1]

Despite the clarion calls for fundamental changes to meet contemporary challenges, public policy is often formed through incremental action. In the words of one academic, "The strategy of incrementalism is one of continual policy readjustments in pursuit of marginally redefined policy goals. Long-term plans are abandoned in favor of short-term political implementation." [2] With some frequency, budgets for specific programs are marginally cut or increased; eligibility criteria are changed; regulations promulgated. Within the bounds of administrative discretion, public managers try to shift resources into areas with the greatest needs and from programs perceived as having less compelling needs. Elected officials attempt to obtain more public resources for their own jurisdictions and to shift resources in response to changing public opinion about social priorities.

In contrast to incrementalism, some rural development experts have argued for a sustained campaign or movement to achieve systemic or institutional changes in addressing the problem of rural competitiveness.[3] This chapter describes a policy development process developed by CGPA which, in combination with strong gubernatorial leadership, has produced substantive policy reform. The process seeks to achieve more than one would expect through incrementalism and creates a nucleus of leadership from which a sustained campaign or movement could emerge.

Governors have many opportunities to develop substantive policy initiatives. Following the first campaign victory, the major issues during the campaign are often developed into a substantive legislative package. Subsequent State of the State addresses set the agenda for the legislative sessions. Governors also avoid the trap of incrementalism by convening commissions, working groups, and task forces to study major (usually controversial) issues and report later with recommendations. Occasionally, convening such groups has "bought time" for governors, which has enabled them to avoid taking a hasty position on a hot issue. In their best use, however, such forums grant governors much more latitude to explore policy alternatives, the opportunity to understand more completely both the history and the complexity of an issue, and the occasion to find common ground for future issue resolution.

In rather broad terms, the CGPA policy development process has tried to provide some of the same structure and focus that have guided the best of these special governors' commissions and study groups. The CGPA policy development process and its academy design evolved since 1984 through the organization's provision of technical assistance to governors' offices and the development of eight State Policy Academies. Because it employs a strategic planning framework, the CGPA process has been called a rational model for collaborative policy development. The CGPA policy development process, which provided the structure for the 1990 and 1992 state policy academies on rural economic development, is presented in box 5-1.[4]

With support from the Aspen Institute, the Ford Foundation and the W.K. Kellogg Foundation, CGPA held the first round of the State Policy Academy on Economic and Community Development in 1990. Through a competitive review process, ten states were selected to participate: Arkansas, California, Iowa, Maine, Michigan, Mississippi, Missouri, North Dakota, Pennsylvania, and Wyoming. One of the most important criteria in this selection process was the demonstration by the governors' offices of a strong commitment to achieve substantive policy changes.

The primary goal of the academy was to provide an opportunity for state policymakers and local leaders to participate in a collaborative policy development process to address their major rural problems. One objective was to assist these state teams, each of which averaged twelve members, to develop specific state legislative proposals to address rural problems that could be submitted by

Box 5-1
The Policy Development Process

10. Monitor Progress and Test Results

9. Implement programs and Policies

8. Build Accountability System

7. Gain Support

6. Select Policy and Program Recommendations

5. Identify Effective Strategies

4. Set Goals and Policy Objectives

3. Assess Problems and Opportunities

2. Scan the Policy Environment

1. Develop Common Vision

their governor at the 1991 state legislative session. Another objective was to help each state team, which included top-level state policymakers, to become a nucleus of people who were conversant with rural issues, committed to addressing them, and possessed of a common vision that could shape subsequent policy development.

The academy was designed to present a roster of experts on important issues in the field of rural development. Unlike a typical workshop or conference, these experts were available to consult individually with each team after their formal presentations. The experts were called faculty. Each team was also given its own meeting room and was assisted in its deliberations by a trained facilitator, who was called a coach. Most academy days included: panels of faculty who presented expert advice on rural issues; sessions that described the CGPA policy development process; and plenty of uninterrupted time for the state teams to discuss, debate and, ultimately, clarify their own rural policy agenda. The academy also provided several opportunities for state teams to present their work to date to other teams, which provided valuable peer review. (See box 5-2 for a brief summary of some of the substantive accomplishments of a few of these state teams.)

The State Policy Academy on Rural Competitiveness in 1992 followed the

Box 5-2

Selective Policy Accomplishments from State Teams Participating in the 1990 Rural Academy

Arkansas: The team considered that its mission was to develop a strategy that would both maintain the unique cultural and historical aspects of rural Arkansas and improve the quality of life for its citizens. Three major achievements were: 1) the creation of a *Rural Advocacy Office and Commission*, which would function as a clearinghouse to connect rural people and businesses with information, assistance, and other necessary resources; 2) an *Expanded Rural Community Self-Help Program*, which in the spring of 1991 was legislatively amended to increase the size of grant awards and increase the population criteria for the program; and 3) a *Small Business Revolving Fund*, to provide modest loans (up to one hundred thousand) to businesses that employ fifty or fewer people.

Iowa: The team focused on three broad themes: 1) Rural Iowa must define its own future. The state's primary role is seen as facilitating local decision making; 2) Partnerships and cooperative arrangements are critical to the future quality and viability of rural communities, businesses, and institutions; and 3) The state's role is as a catalyst for others, rather than as the direct and sole provider of a particular service. Several strategies merit attention: the *Rural Community Leadership Program* that provides seed money, technical assistance and training to communities; *Networking Rural Growth Industries*: in one case with a Technology Center to provide training, technology development and transfer, and network services to participating companies; *Bankers' Workshops on Financing Rural Businesses*; and *Promoting Entrepreneurship* to provide a supportive culture for risk taking among adults now operating businesses and those who are potential entrepreneurs.

Maine: The team sought to maintain the vitality and character of its rural communities. One of its strategies was to assist existing and new businesses to become more expansion oriented by developing *Entrepreneurial Account Executives*, which was intended to help rural businesses improve their access to talent, skill, and capital, and reduce governmental obstacles. Another strategy was to extend *"Maine Street '90,"* which was a private-public partnership focusing on increasing community spirit and activity within Maine towns.

North Dakota: The team, lead by the Governor's Chief of Staff, was determined to develop a comprehensive economic development plan. Its recommendations included: incentives for diversified economic growth; targeting services toward agricultural diversification; local capacity building; economic development education; targeted business recruitment; enhancement of minority and women's business development; strengthening and focusing the economic development functions within state government; and enhancing collaboration between the resources of higher education and the state economic development delivery system. This package was strongly endorsed by Governor Sinner, became the focus of his 1991 State of the State Address, and was enacted by the legislature in the spring of 1991.

Features of this legislation that related to rural entrepreneurship and business development included: a *Primary Sector Development Fund*, a new $7 million program to provide capital for businesses engaged in value-added agriculture, energy by-product development, and exported services; *Science and Technology* investments to investigate and research various value-added opportunities; *Regional Centers* to provide technical assistance to primary sector business development; *Dakota Spirit*, which is a program to assist communities in undertaking economic development projects, community assessment, goal setting, and other self-help activities; a new and special program to assist *Minority and Women-owned Businesses*; and *Banker Training*, a continuing education program for bank lenders to facilitate the availability of financing for small and new businesses.

Source: Mark G. Popovich, *New Businesses, Entrepreneurship, and Rural Development: State Policies and Generating Rural Growth from Within*, (January 1993), CGPA, 400 North Capitol Street, Suite 390, Washington, D.C. 20001; 202.624.5386. Mr. Popovich was the project director for the 1990 State Policy Academy for Rural Economic and Community Development.

same CGPA model, but placed special emphasis on efforts to address the needs of economically distressed rural places and people. It was also designed to provide state governments with an opportunity to prepare for the formation of State Rural Development Councils by providing strategic planning for subsequent state policy development and SRDC program implementation. The states selected to attend this policy academy were California, Hawaii, Idaho, Nebraska, New Mexico, and Virginia. (See box 5-4 for a summary of their accomplishments.)

The experiences of the states involved in both academies may provide some general guidance to the state policymakers seeking different approaches in improving rural competitiveness. The CGPA policy development process provided a structured approach to problem solving and a group process for making rational decisions about priorities. The steps were used to *guide*, but not limit, the work of the state teams. Often the teams would leave a contentious topic and move on to discuss another topic or another step in the process. It was also an *iterative* rather than linear process. For example, a working group of one of the teams worked very hard during the summer to produce a superior environmental scan, but, after a review by the full team, it became apparent that important information was lacking.

Some of the participants, especially those who defined themselves as task oriented, were frustrated by such an elusive process. Success with this type of group process requires extraordinary amounts of energy and patience, the ability to listen closely to one's colleagues, and great faith that the resulting product will justify such hard work.

Developing a Common Vision

The initial focus of the state teams was to develop a common vision that described what they wanted for the rural communities of their states. Vision statements can be very powerful in unifying group members within a common agenda and in motivating people to work toward that agenda. Indeed, it is difficult to conceive of a sustained campaign or movement for rural development, or any other cause, that fails to project a strong shared vision. Here is the definition of vision that CGPA presented, which originated at the Stanford Business School:

> Vision is the ability to see the potential in, or necessity of, opportunities right in front of you. And, just as important, it is the courage, skills, passionate conviction, and relentless persistence to actually make it happen.....
> Vision isn't forecasting the future; it is creating the future by taking action in the present.[5]

The vision statements developed by the state teams were heartfelt, spirited, pictorial, intuitive, and poetic. During one team sharing session, the lights were dimmed and the Hawaii team members were asked to close their eyes while they heard a dramatic reading of a powerful vision statement for Idaho rural communities. It was stirring. (See box 5-3 for the Idaho vision statement.)

Obviously some of that initial work on their vision statements enabled the team members to learn to work with and trust one another, to provide some common vocabulary, to begin a collaborative process, and to overcome past agency turf battles and professional identifications. Equally important, this initial exercise helped each team to establish its unifying theme and mission (which later helped to sustain it when it became laden with conflict and fatigue).

Scan the Policy Environment

An environmental scan is a comprehensive inventory of information about the economic, social, and political features that define the policy environment. Important elements of history, culture, and physical conditions are also features of a good environmental scan. The following is the way CGPA identified the key elements of an environmental scan:

Assessments of trends and conditions in these areas related to rural economic development: employment, income, economic base (farm, manufacturing, and service industries), human resources base, financial base, health and safety, infrastructure and amenities, institutions (including government), political history, population affected, current development strategies (including the type and distribution of services, access to rural areas, public and private sector roles, provider characteristics and effectiveness, and barriers to success), and the predominant values/philosophy/attitudes of community leaders, business, and general populace;

Descriptions of the status of rural economies in the state, including data that describes the extent and severity of the aforementioned factors; and

Projections of how recent trends, if continued, would affect rural issues, problems, and proposed strategies to promote rural competitiveness.

This was an incredible amount of work, but this research often paid handsome dividends later. The North Dakota team leader, Chuck Fleming, the governor's chief of staff, responded to CGPA's guidelines by requesting that each state department assume responsibility for finding the appropriate information

Box 5-3
A Vision of Rural Idaho

PEOPLE—*We see a rural Idaho where*: Human dignity is a priority, people are the focus, and youth is a particularly vital resource, services are available to meet lifelong basic human needs, and there are opportunities for all individuals to thrive regardless of physical ability, income, race, or culture.

ENVIRONMENT—*We see a rural Idaho where*: Idaho's rugged beautiful land molds our character, and our economic and environmental needs are balanced through thoughtful, sustainable use of our national resources; we are willing and able to share Idaho's recreational opportunities and cultural treasures with visitors; and there are untouched, natural places where wildlife thrives and the human spirit is lifted.

ECONOMY—*We see a rural Idaho where*: The economy is vibrant and offers opportunities for agricultural, natural resource, manufacturing and service industries; entrepreneurship is encouraged; ongoing success in the global marketplace is supported by state-of-the-art communications systems and technology; there is a well-maintained, statewide transportation network; and there are meaningful jobs offering incomes to sustain a preferred standard of living and quality of life.

and data. As a result of this herculean effort, each North Dakota team member arriving at the first academy session in 1990 had a notebook stuffed with information about the rural economies in North Dakota.

This compiled database served several important functions. The environmental scan provided encyclopedic information to the full team. It dispelled common myths entertained by some of the team members about various industries in the state. Whenever a dispute over a fact threatened to dominate the discussion, Fleming would direct the participants to "Look it up in the Blue Book." It provided a reality-based foundation for the subsequent discussions about policy options and economic development strategies.

This powerful example helped motivate the state teams in the 1992 academy to invest the time and effort to provide good environmental scans for their own states. Another valuable asset in explaining the concept of an environmental scan was the recent work by Richard Gardner, *Rural Profile of Idaho*

EDUCATION—*We see a rural Idaho where*: An educational system encourages and provides affordable and accessible opportunities for lifelong learning; students of all ages are prepared to succeed in a global environment; educational systems are responsive to diverse industry needs and community values; and the family is an active partner in education.

GOVERNMENT—*We see a rural Idaho where*: Responsive government serves its citizens; citizens are informed and passionately involved in decision making; leaders emerge from all walks of life and all segments of the community; and effective public/private partnerships flourish.

VALUES—*We see a rural Idaho where*: Our values are revered and passed on to our children; we use our heritage to create our future; we honor family and value cultural diversity; we encourage artistic expression; productivity is a way of life; we view adversity as a challenge; and the responsibilities of citizenship are accepted by all, and the benefits are accessible to all.

Source: Idaho team, approved 5/28/92.

(1990), and his presentations at the Team Leaders Meeting and at the first academy session. Gardner, who served as the coach/facilitator for the North Dakota team in 1990 and was the Idaho team leader in the 1992 academy, had written a report that conveyed very important information in an accessible format (by using clear graphics, thoughtful headings, and good designs).

The moral of this story is that hard facts are superior to common myths, at least as the basis for making policy decisions. The proscription that follows is that *state governments should collect, analyze, and produce economic data about its major industries and sectors, which could be organized and shared with community leaders on a regional basis*. Equally significant, rural advocates may benefit from investing much more effort in learning about their regional and local economies. State legislators, who are often not included early enough in the policy development process, would also appreciate having solid information and analysis about rural economies.

Assess Problems and Opportunities

An exceedingly difficult step in this process was that of objectively evaluating both the problems and opportunities of rural communities. "A problem well stated," said Charles F. Kettering, "is a problem half-solved." Many of the participants had had experience with the SWOT technique (Strengths, Weaknesses, Opportunities, and Threats) as a method for directing critical thinking. Some participants found that using the concept of comparative advantage helped them identify the strengths and potential opportunities of rural communities. This analysis was important to designing effective strategies; (it was also a positive experience for many since the weaknesses and problems of rural communities had dominated their attention on a daily basis).

To guide the state teams, CGPA presented these basic questions:

- What are the major problems and opportunities?

- Who is affected by these problems and who could benefit from potential opportunities?

- How serious are these problems and how significant could these opportunities become?

- Will outcomes be better or worse in the future if recent trends continue?

- What are the underlying causes for major problems?

- What are the priorities among both problems and opportunities?[6]

Set Goals and Policy Objectives

Some strategic planning guides begin with goal setting. CGPA has found that working through the above steps develops broad consensus and prepares the group for an informed, enriched discussion about goals. The teams were encouraged to set broad policy goals and then develop specific outcome-oriented objectives. The discrete objectives are particularly important to set clear direction and to develop a responsible accountability system. Teams were encouraged to select criteria for setting priorities and, ultimately, to establish priorities for both goals and objectives.

Identify Effective Strategies

Strategies to improve rural competitiveness was the central theme of the policy academy. Potential strategies surfaced early for some teams as they worked through the initial steps of this policy development process. Strategies were developed later by other teams after the participants had listened to presenters and had studied the descriptions of other states' programs.[7]

CGPA encouraged brainstorming sessions (such as those used by the Nestbuilders of Custer County, as described in chapter 4) to stimulate creative ideas and unconventional approaches. Voluminous materials on state and rural economic development programs were distributed to the participants. Team-sharing sessions were held so that participants could learn from one another. In addition, CGPA recommended that each team evaluate existing programs in its state to learn more about what works well, select among the strategies and programs identified earlier, test each for plausibility and feasibility, and then set priorities.

Gain Support

The state teams participated in this academy because their governors had expressed a commitment to this process. Most of the team leaders were members of the governors' policy staff, managed a major state agency, or held cabinet rank. The participants knew only too well the cliché: "The governor proposes, and the legislature disposes." Hence, the teams knew that they had to develop a much broader political strategy to elicit support among state legislators and potential allies.

The following are a few observations drawn from their deliberations on how to gain support for strategies to improve rural competitiveness:

- Most participants felt strongly that government has had and has a moral responsibility to preserve places; but they did not think that the moral claim, by itself, would be effective in reestablishing the federal government's role in promoting rural development. In general, they felt that history, the moral claim, or most traditional arguments were not going to convince enough members of Congress to increase substantially federal resources for rural development. They were slightly more optimistic that these arguments, if presented skillfully, could be persuasive in shifting resources within state government.

- Few participants thought that the efficiency arguments for investing in regional economies, which are summarized in chapter 2, would be an effective argument in their state capitals. Some may have harbored their own doubts that public investments would be made strategically to improve the regional or state economies. Others, presumably, felt that the investment concept — wisely spending more today will save money and/or produce handsome benefits later — had become an overused, and hence devalued, currency in state government.

- Most participants thought that a combination of the moral claim and sensible appeals of rational self-interest to the general public would make the strongest arguments for major initiatives to improve rural competitiveness. In fact, several teams worked hard to develop strategies that would effectively "tell the story" about the problems and opportunities of their rural communities through the media to engender broader public support for new initiatives.

A different conceptual approach to gaining support for rural economies merits brief mention, although it will be considered heretical by some rural development experts. The argument is that advocacy for rural development has become marginalized politically and is either ignored by the public or is perceived as special pleading by Congress and many state legislatures. A more effective political strategy, according to this view, is to resolve the set of responsibilities that should be assumed by the federal, state, and local governments. Clarification of that allows state governments to develop a more realistic approach toward the services it provides and how it should work with regional and local jurisdictions. This "sorting out" approach would effectively scrutinize existing institutions and organizations, posing a threat to some of them, and force systemic changes. Nevertheless, it could lead to a more rational structure for providing public services.[8]

As a modest step in this direction, a suggestion has been made that economic development activities be funded on a regional basis, thereby forging tighter bonds between urban and rural areas. By directing the debate to the topic of *place*, this approach forms powerful alliances between rural communities and nearby cities. (The Oregon regional strategies initiative described in chapter 4 may provide some practical guidance to those intrigued with this idea.) Daniel Kemmis made this sensible recommendation in his thoughtful book, *Community and the Politics of Place*:

> As rural life is threatened more and more severely by international markets, by technological dislocations and corporate domination, it may be time for a reassessment of the relationship between cities and their rural environs. It may well be that neither towns nor farms can thrive in the way they would prefer until they turn their attention more directly to each other, realizing that they are mutually complementary parts of the enterprise of

inhabiting a particular place—whether that place be called a bioregion, a city-state, or a *polis*. As a rule, we come closer to this way of thinking in the economic than in the political sphere.[9]

Build Accountability Systems

Duncan Wyse, the executive director of the Oregon Progress Board, made a presentation at the second academy session about the use of benchmarks to monitor government programs and social progress. Oregon's work is in the forefront in this regard.[10]

In addition, CGPA presented these guiding principles for building an accountability system:

• Determine the indicators of success;

• Involve data generators in system design;

• Organize to gather appropriate data;

• Develop incentives or mandates for data collection and reporting; and

• Collect and analyze data.

Implement Programs and Policies

Implementation is quite different than planning. Implementation means making the plans work. CGPA recommended that the state teams develop work plans, timetables, and specific assignments to implement their strategies. Unforeseen obstacles often emerge during the implementation phase, so CGPA advised that the teams periodically meet to clarify expected results, resolve residual conflicts between existing and new objectives, and target priorities for strategic resource allocation.

Monitor Progress and Test Results

The final step in this policy development process emphasized that the policy environment and major problems are volatile. As they change, both objectives and strategies must be revised accordingly. Special attention should be given to the information from accountability systems so that revised priorities are based on meaningful results. Hence, implementation timetables have to be revised periodically. (See box 5-4.)

Box 5-4

Summary of Accomplishments of States in the 1992 State Policy Academy on Rural Competitiveness

California—The Governor's Task Force on Rural Competitiveness, which was the traveling team for the academy, followed Governor Wilson's direction to obtain true grassroots input. The Task Force convened the Rural Roundtable and held eight Rural Town Hall meetings throughout the state. This opened the process to more than two thousand participants and as many divergent groups as possible. Following these sessions, the Task Force developed policy recommendations for the governor and the legislature.

Hawaii—The academy team produced excellent work before the second academy session, but was impressed with the outreach effort developed by the California team and decided to promote greater public involvement in its process. The working product set important directions for developing the comparative advantages of the rural areas for economic development while respecting cultural traditions and values. Unfortunately, the team's leadership was diverted to other tasks, such as responding to the devastation caused by Hurricane Iniki; as a result, the academy-directed work was temporarily halted last fall.

Idaho—The academy team has become the nucleus of the State Rural Development Council, and its work provided a clear, strategic direction for the council's initial activity. In addition, Richard Gardner, the Idaho team leader, became the first executive director of the SDRC.

CODA

Policy experts are frequently preoccupied with trying to "fix" social problems by tinkering at the margins. They labor in good faith for an incremental reform today and another tomorrow. Many who teach political science and public policy are steeped in the narrow confines of incrementalism. Society is fortunate to benefit from their contribution, but we are also fortunate to have forceful advocates and dreamers. It is they who push the policy experts and others to see a bigger picture, think about larger questions, and remind all of us that some of the constraints that limit our hopes could actually be changed.

Nebraska—Its academy team, which included the lieutenant governor, had developed a much stronger consensus on its approach, had refined some of its more innovative economic development strategies, and had presented a series of recommendations to Governor Nelson. Don Macke, one of its team members, later became the executive director of the Nebraska State Rural Development Council.

New Mexico—To obtain broad representation of varied rural constituencies throughout the state, twenty-one people participated in the academy sessions. The team became the nucleus of the New Mexico Rural Development Response Council. By virtue of its academy-directed work, the full academy team became the strategic planning subcommittee for the newly formed SRDC.

Virginia—Its academy team used its work to develop a new strategic plan for its state rural development program. It also recommended budget items before the 1993 state legislative session and briefed the governor in January 1993 on its work and objectives. It expects to publish a compendium document, *A Blueprint for Rural Virginia*, in the summer of 1993 that presents priorities, strategies, and background material.

Often, however, their grand vision lacks the structure and design required to produce meaningful change.

The CGPA policy academy has sought to capture the best of both approaches. We began by assisting the state teams in articulating the vision they had for the rural communities in their states. Here is the way Peter Senge explained the power of visioning as a prelude to action and change:

> A shared vision is not an idea. It is not even an important idea such as freedom. It is, rather, a force in people's hearts, a force of impressive power. It may be inspired by an idea, but once it goes further — if it is compelling

enough to acquire the support of more than one person — then it is no longer an abstraction. It is palpable. People begin to see it as if it exists. Few, if any, forces in human affairs are as powerful as shared vision.[11]

The organizing precept of this academy was that state policymakers wanted and needed to learn more about their rural economies and how they would have to adapt to global competition to maintain the future viability of rural communities. The participants in these policy academies had the benefit of a good deal of research on state and rural economic development policies and programs. The bulk of chapter 4 was presented in a different form during the two 1992 academy sessions.

The efforts of these state teams have had an immediate impact in shaping state policy. The 1991 economic development legislation in North Dakota made major changes and captured headlines. The innovative approaches in Nebraska may not receive as much public attention, but they also will have a real, meaningful impact on their rural workers, their families, and their communities. Similarly, the hard work of the New Mexico and Idaho teams provided an excellent beginning and direction for their State Rural Development Councils. The California team convened roundtable sessions in rural areas throughout the state to learn more about regional challenges and used these findings to make policy recommendations to the governor. The Virginia team developed a new strategic plan for rural development. The Hawaii team effort will also make a contribution to state policy debates and help focus attention on the problems and opportunities of the rural people and rural communities of the state. Some of the legislative proposals developed by state teams have been endorsed by their governors and may be enacted by their state legislatures.

The CGPA policy academy brought top policymakers together to work toward making systemic changes in state policies. This objective involves more than simply assisting a state team to research and draft a legislative package for the governor's office. It entails building a foundation of knowledge, developing analytical skills to diagnose complex issues and to evaluate various policy options, providing professional and organizational skills to enhance the ability of participants to be effective agents of change, and presenting a structured opportunity for participants to "expand their ability to create." [12]

Perhaps the lasting contribution of this state policy academy has been the opportunity to work closely with people who are committed to addressing important rural issues, and share a vocabulary, a perspective on policy development, and a set of common experiences. Once again, Peter Senge has captured the social magic of working collegially toward a common goal:

Most of us at one time or another have been part of a great "team," a group of people who functioned together in an extraordinary way — who trusted one another, who complemented each others' strengths and compensated for each others' limitations, who had common goals that were larger than individual goals, and who produced extraordinary results. I have met many people who have experienced this sort of profound teamwork.... Many say that they have spent much of their life looking for that experience again.[13]

Throughout their professional careers, the participants of these academies — even as their duties and responsibilities change — will remain leaders in state policy debates about rural communities. In a modest way, the CGPA policy academies helped produce part of the leadership cadre for rural America.

Notes:

1. As quoted by Rosabeth Moss Kanter, *The Change Masters: Innovation and Entrepreneurship in the American Corporation*, (New York: Simon & Schuster, 1984), 17.

2. Paul R. Schulman, "Nonincremental Policy Making: Notes Toward an Alternative Paradigm," *The American Political Science Review* 49, no.4 (December 1975): 1354.

3. See Ronald R. Ferguson and DeWitt John, *Developing Rural America for 21st Century Competitiveness: The Emerging Movement and the Critical Ideas Behind Best Practices*, Working Draft. (Washington, D.C.: The Aspen Institute, forthcoming).

4. The CGPA strategic policy development process and its academy design have both evolved since 1984 through the organization's work with more than thirty-five states that sent teams to participate in state policy academies on topics such as preventing teen pregnancy, enhancing work force literacy, preventing school dropouts, and assisting families and children that are at risk. The initial model for this approach was derived from the strategic planning approach used by corporations and other large organizations during the 1970s and 1980s. Many of its key features were described in *Thinking Strategically: A Primer for Public Leaders* by Susan Walter and Pat Choate (CSPA, 1984) and in *Strategic Policy for the Nation's Governors*, Lauren Cook, ed. (CGPA, 1990). The policy development process has also been used through CGPA's technical assistance program to assist governors' policy advisors. For another perspective on these process issues, see *Gearing Up for Success: Organizing a State for Rural Development* by David W. Sears, John M. Redman, Richard L. Gardner, and Stephen J. Adams, (Washington, D.C.: Aspen Institute, 1992). The Corporation for Enterprise Development, the National Governors' Association, and the USDA's Economic Research Service and Extension Service collaborated on both State Policy Academies. In addition, the Western Governors' Association collaborated on the 1990 Academy; also Jobs for the Future and USDA's Rural Development Administration collaborated on the 1992 Academy.

5. As quoted by North Dakota 2000 Committee, in *Vision 2000; Kick-Off Report*, Bismarck, North Dakota, March 1990, p.8.

6. CGPA also provided the participants with a paper, "Diagnosing: Understanding Rural Development Problems and Opportunities" by Roger J. Vaughan, which posed additional analytical questions and suggestions for critical evaluation of rural economies.

7. An important discussion occurred during one of the workshops following a presentation about the public-private model being developed in Kansas and Kentucky state governments. Some of the participants asked questions about the interests and motivations of the business leaders who were involved in "steering" the course for state economic development programs: specifically, was the private-sector agenda the same as the public purpose for these programs? How much private-sector involvement was appropriate in directing public programs? Would such public-private partnerships result in more or less accountability for the expenditure of public funds?

8. See Alice M. Rivlin, *Reviving the American Dream: The Economy, the States & the Federal Government*, (Washington, D.C.: Brookings, 1992).

9. Daniel Kemmis, *Community and the Politics of Place*, (Norman, Okla.: University of Oklahoma Press, 1990), 124; see also Graham S. Toft, "Rurban Development," *Entrepreneurial Economy Review* 8, no.4 (January-February 1990): 13-19.

10. Those interested in accountability and benchmarks in state government should obtain *Oregon Benchmarks: Standards for Measuring Statewide Progress and Government Performance*, Oregon Progress Board, 775 Summer Street, N.E., Salem, Oregon 97310; 503.373.1220. For a survey of research that has evaluated economic development programs, see Timothy J. Bartnik, *Who Benefits from State and Local Economic Development Policies?* Kalamazoo, Michigan: W.E. Upjohn Institute for Employment Research, 1991; and for assistance in designing evaluation measures, see Harry P. Hatry, Mark Fall, Thomas O. Singer, and E. Blaine Liner, *Monitoring the Outcomes of Economic Development Programs: A Manual*, (Washington, D.C: Urban Institute Press, 1990).

11. Peter Senge, *The Fifth Discipline: The Art and Practice of the Learning Organization* (New York: Currency/Doubleday, 1990), 206.

12. This is Peter Senge's phrase for what a "learning organization" allows its workers to do.

13. Ibid., 4.

The Economic Challenqe Revisited

The essential point about change is this: Our ability to sustain a stable, democratic and prosperous society depends on our capacity to change. It depends on all of us having the courage to change — even when change is uncomfortable, even when there is resistance to change and even when some of the consequences of change are unknown. We cannot cling to the past. In a democratic society, the status quo is the enemy of stability, not his friend.   — Governor Booth Gardner[1]

In writing about the concepts of economic development theorists during the last two centuries, W.W.Rostow referred to "the Chinese expression of the concept of crisis as embracing the characters of both danger and opportunity." [2] This may be an apt description of rural America today. Despite its noble past, the current problems and longer-term trends represent serious threats to the economic viability of many rural communities. But rural communities also have reservoirs of great strength, tenacity, and civic commitment. The serious challenges of today could become the opportunities for a better tomorrow.

The American economy consists of a range of activities and functions. At the highest end, firms are producing high value-added goods and services, usually with advanced technology and highly skilled workers, that compete successfully in global markets. At the lowest end, firms produce or process raw materials to serve the consumers in local markets. To maintain a rising national standard of living, every aspect of the national economy must seek to achieve greater productivity of all inputs: labor, land (natural resources), and capital in its various forms. Recall the definition of economic competitiveness presented in chapter 1: "our ability to produce goods and services that meet the test of international markets while our citizens enjoy a standard of living that is both rising and sustainable."[3]

The productivity challenge for the national economy has two geographical weak links: rural America and inner-city neighborhoods. It is urgent that they become full partners in the national restructuring that will lead to future prosperity. Both need special educational assistance to train their youth for future jobs. Both need state and federal assistance to develop sufficient public infrastructure to support social and economic stability. Both have been neglected for many years. And the continued neglect of both represents an unnecessary burden on the rest of the economy, as well as the denial of meaningful opportunity for those kept on the sidelines, apart from the mainstream economy.

Investment in human capital is likely to be the best economic development strategy for both areas in improving the health and welfare of their residents, in raising skill levels and career aspirations, and in preparing them to integrate into the mainstream economy. Beyond these common approaches, the fundamental differences in population density and access to vibrant urban economies are likely to require different economic development strategies.[4] But the collaborative policy development process described in chapter 5 — assessing strengths and weaknesses, devising broad strategies, coordinating and redirecting community resources, and initiating efforts to overcome past disadvantages — could be used by state policymakers and community leaders from both areas.

As the states struggle through their own process of designing initiatives to promote rural competitiveness, it may be helpful to return to the definition of economic development provided in the third chapter — *Economic development is the process of facilitating economic growth and the development of an adaptive capacity to sustain a higher level of activity in the future from its own resources.* Recruitment of firms — either the old pattern of seeking branch plants or the more recent version of attracting information-intensive functions such as telemarketing, customer support, mail-order fulfillment, or data entry — is not unimportant. It has been, after all, a major strategy and is intuitively logical. Moreover, as long as public officials are pushed by the electoral cycle to maintain a short-term focus, recruitment efforts will be continued. Recruitment activities should not, however, be the only strategy taken by rural community leaders to improve their economies.

The broad strategies described in chapter 4 may be more effective in the long term in achieving rural competitiveness than traditional recruitment activities. State governments should work closely with rural communities, and both should make social investments in those strategies that develop the capacity to sustain a higher level of economic activity in the future from their communities' own resources.

In a globally competitive environment, the development capacity of any community resides in its education system, its workers' skills, its communication technologies, its physical and social infrastructure, and its leadership. These are the development capacities that will provide the adaptive ability of communities to compete, innovate, and succeed economically in the future.[5]

Many rural communities will continue to face difficult challenges in the years ahead. Some, alas, may continue to lose population, employment, and their young people who will drift off, reluctantly perhaps, in search of career and social opportunities. The trend of population moving from rural areas has been a century-long trend, with the exception of the 1970s, and may well continue, driven by powerful external forces beyond the scope of most public interventions. During the nineteenth century, for example, many of the western mining towns were no longer economically viable after the precious metals were extracted. Efforts to prevent their collapse would have imposed far higher social costs than the social benefits derived from preservation.

Rural economies based on natural resources industries are subject to intensive global competition; they have less control over their collective fate in the turbulent future than those communities able to develop their adaptive capacity to compete in diversified economic sectors. Private and public investments made to adapt to new economic imperatives to create rural competitiveness would provide generous social benefits and improve the economic viability of many rural communities.

Inertia is a powerful force. Even when ineffective, the old ways of doing things provide great comfort. In Osha Gray Davidson's thoughtful book, *Broken Heartland: The Rise of America's Rural Ghetto*, he told this story about the resistance of rural Iowans to quick changes of any kind:

> A retired farmer once told me that his father was the first person in the area to try raising soybeans back in the early part of this century, when corn was the undisputed king.
>
> "It probably took quite a while to catch on," I remarked.
>
> "Oh, no," he assured me. "Why, some of the neighbors were giving the new crop a try just six or seven years later." [6]

The primary objective of this book is to clarify for state policymakers the economic challenge that rural economies face and to offer some policy options. A secondary objective was to make the argument that, in response to this challenge, state governments and rural organizations and institutions must be flexible and able to change in response to adversity. The challenge is so great and resources so limited that those concerned about the economic viability of rural communities in this country must be prepared to form collaborations and search for new policy approaches. Working together, even with a powerful, shared vision, is hard work and requires sustained commitment.[7]

Some of rural America's leadership will be receptive to this message (others will be threatened by it), but how will those respond who live and work in rural America? Will they embrace change with all of its uncertainties? Will they accept the gradual loss of their natural resource-based employment and prepare themselves for the jobs of the future? Will their organizations be flexible and resilient?

For the purpose of contrasting images, reflect upon the Davidson story of farmers willing to try a new crop after just six or seven years of observation — which *does* portray the conservative culture in many rural communities. Then compare that conservative culture with this description of how our world is rapidly shrinking and changing:

> The rate of change is speeding up in an amazing way. If we pretend that the time elapsed since the Southern ape man appeared on planet Earth some five million years ago and today has been a single supermonth, where every second represents two years, the "future compression" problem comes into clear focus.
>
> In our supermonth, humankind spends almost the entire 30 days as a hunter/gatherer. It is only in the last one-and-a-half hours of the supermonth that towns and agriculture have arisen. The last four minutes are the Renaissance, and the last 90-second segment represents the Industrial Revolution. Amazingly, it is only the last 15 seconds that relates to transistors, satellites, fiber optics, electronic switches, color television, biotechnology, and artificial intelligence. In physics, when acceleration accelerates, it is called *jerk*. In our modern information age, the time differential of change is speeding up and "jerking" us into the future.[8]

The communities of rural America are, today, in fierce competition with the rest of the globe for employment, income, and economic viability. Some of the external forces that will determine the fate of rural communities in this nation are clearly beyond our control. But state policymakers working in concert with the leaders of rural communities can design effective strategies to promote rural competitiveness. Many of the broad economic development strategies summarized in chapter 4 could be adapted to fit the unique political and social context of state and local governments. The policy development process described in chapter 5 may provide some guidance to those committed to making new strategies work effectively.

The nation's governors and their policy advisors have a unique opportunity to promote rural competitiveness. The success of any state in promoting rural competitiveness will require collaboration, innovation, and a commitment to change — perhaps to a degree seldom experienced. The fate of rural families and their communities will rest, to a very large extent, upon the vision and bold action of state policymakers and their own community leaders.

Notes:

1. 1. Booth Gardner, "A Washington Farewell," *State Government News* (Lexington, Ky.: Council of State Governments, April 1993), 16; the article was excerpted from his 1993 State of the State address. Booth Gardner was governor of Washington for eight years.

2. See also W. W. Rostow, *Theorists of Economic Growth from David Hume to the Present* (New York: Oxford University Press, 1990), 389.

3. Laura D'Andrea Tyson, *Who's Bashing Whom? Trade Conflict in High-Technology Industries*, (Washington, D.C.: Institute for International Economics, 1992), 1.

4. For one of the better articles that summarizes the problems of innercity residents and proposes strategies to address them, see John D. Kasarda, "City Jobs and Residents on a Collision Course: The Urban Underclass Dilemma," *Economic Development Quarterly* 4 no.4 (November 1990): 313-319.

5. In his book, *The Power Economy: Building an Economy That Works*, (Boston: Little, Brown, 1985), John Oliver Wilson wrote that:

> Comparative economic advantage has taken on a new meaning. This newer concept replaces the traditional criteria "with such elements as human creative power, foresight, a highly educated work force, organizational talent, the ability to choose, and the ability to adapt. Moreover, these attributes are not conceived of as natural endowments but as qualities achieved through public policies such as education, organized research, and investment in social overhead capital.

> Wilson was quoting from Chalmers Johnson, "The Idea of Industrial Policy," in *Industrial Policy Debate*, Chalmers Johnson, ed. (San Francisco: Institute for Contemporary Studies, 1984), 8.

6. Osha Gray Davidson, *Broken Heartland: The Rise of America's Rural Ghetto* (New York: Anchor Books/Doubleday, 1990), 9-10.

7. For constructive advice, see John M. Bryson and Barbara C. Crosby, *Leadership for the Common Good: Tackling Public Problems in a Shared-Power World*, (San Francisco: Jossey-Bass, 1992); for a scholarly explanation of the reason that this challenge is so difficult, see Mancur Olson, *The Rise and Decline of Nations: Economic Growth, Stagflation, and Social Rigidities*, (New Haven: Yale University Press, 1982).

8. Joseph N. Pelton, "The Globalization of Universal Telecommunications Services," *Universal Telephone Service: Ready for the 21st Century?* (Queenstown, Md.: Institute for Information Studies, 1991), 142.

SELECTED BIBLIOGRAPHY

Adams, Stephen J. *The Productivity Imperative and the New Maine Economy*. Augusta: Maine State Planning Office, April 1990.

Advisory Commission on Intergovernmental Relations. *State and Local Initiatives on Productivity, Technology, and Innovation: Enhancing a National Resource for International Competitiveness*. Washington, D.C.: Advisory Commission on Intergovernmental Relations, May 1990.

Ayres, Janet, Robert Cole, Clair Hein, Stuart Huntington, Wayne Kobberdahl, Wanda Leonard, and Dale Zetocha. *Take Charge: Economic Development in Small Communities*. Ames, Iowa: North Central Regional Center for Rural Development, 1990.

Barber, Marian. *County Economic Development in the 1990's: Report on a NACCED Survey*. Washington, D.C.: National Association for County Community Economic Development, 1991.

Barlett, Donald L., and James B. Steele. *America: What Went Wrong?* Kansas City, Mo.: Andrews and McMeel, 1992.

Berry, Wendell. *The Gift of Good Land*. San Francisco: North Point Press, 1981.

Blinder, Alan S. *Maintaining Competitiveness with High Wages*. San Francisco: International Center for Economic Growth, 1992.

Bollier, David, James Harvey, and Hilary Pennington. *Pioneers of Progress: Policy Entrepreneurs and Community Development*. Somerville, Mass.: Jobs for the Future, 1991.

Bosworth, Brian. "State Strategies for Manufacturing Modernization." In *Excellence at Work: Policy Option Papers*. Kalamazoo, Mich.: W. E. Upjohn Institute for Employment Research, 1992.

Brown, David L., J. Norman Reid, Herman Bluestone, David A. McGranahan, and Sara M. Mazie, eds. *Rural Economic Development in the 1980's: Prospects for the Future*. Washington, D.C.: Economic Research Service, U.S. Department of Agriculture, 1988.

Buss, Terry E., and Roger J. Vaughan. *On the Rebound: Helping Workers Cope with Plant Closings*. Washington, D.C.: Council of State Policy and Planning Agencies, 1988.

Center on Budget and Policy Priorities. *Fulfilling Work's Promise: Policies to Increase Incomes of the Rural Working Poor*. Washington, D.C.: Center on Budget and Policy Priorities, 1990.

Chynoweth, Judith K., Lauren Cook, Michael D. Campbell, and Barbara R. Dyer. *Experiments in Systems Change: States Implement Family Policy*. Final Report to the Ford Foundation and United Way of America. Washington, D.C.: Council of Governors' Policy Advisors, September 1992.

Cook, Lauren, ed. *Strategic Policy for the Nation's Governors: Organizing for Effective Policy Development and Implementation*, 3d ed. Washington, D.C.: Council of Governors' Policy Advisors, 1990.

Cornman, John N., and Barbara K. Kincaid. *Lessons from Rural America: a case history*. Cabin John, Md.: Seven Locks Press, 1984.

Corporation for Enterprise Development. *The Entrepreneurial Economy Review* 9 no. 1 (Spring 1991).

Corporation for Enterprise Development. *The Entrepreneurial Economy Review* 6 no. 1 (July/August 1987).

Cortright, Joseph. *Old World New Ideas: Business Assistance Lessons from Europe.* Seattle: Northwest Policy Center, 1990.

Crittenden, Ann. *Killing the Sacred Cows: Bold Ideas for a New Economy.* New York: Penguin Books, 1992.

Cyert, Richard M., and David C. Mowery, eds. *Technology and Employment: Innovation and Growth in the U.S. Economy.* Washington, D.C.: National Academy Press, 1987.

Denison, Edward F. *Trends in American Economic Growth,* 1919-1982. Washington, D.C.: The Brookings Institution, 1985.

Dertouzos, Michael L., Richard K. Lester, and Robert M. Solow. *Made in America: Regaining the Productive Edge.* Cambridge: MIT Press, 1989.

Drucker, Peter F. *Post Capitalist Society.* New York: Harper Collins, 1993.

Duncan, Cynthia, ed. *Rural Poverty in America.* New York: Auburn House, 1992.

Economic Research Service. *Education and Rural Development: Strategies for the 1990s.* ERS Staff Report No. AGES 9153, Washington: Agriculture and Rural Economy Division, Economic Research Service, U.S. Department of Agriculture, September 1991.

Economic Research Service. *Infrastructure Investment and Economic Development.* Staff Report No. AGES 9069, Washington: Agriculture and Rural Economy Division, Economic Research Service, U.S. Department of Agriculture, December 1990.

Farr, Cheryl A., ed. *Shaping the Local Economy: Current Perspectives on Economic Development.* Washington, D.C.: International City Management Association, 1984.

Fitchen, Janet M. *Endangered Spaces, Enduring Places: Change, Identity, and Survival in Rural America.* Boulder, Colo.: Westview Press, 1991.

Flora, Jan L., James J. Chriss, Eddie Gale, Gary P. Green, Frederick E. Smith, and Cornelia Flora. *From the Grassroots: Profiles of 103 Rural Self-Development Projects.* Washington, D.C.: Economic Research Service, U.S. Department of Agriculture, 1991.

Galbraith, John Kenneth. *Economics in Perspective: A Critical History.* Boston: Houghton Mifflin, 1987.

Gardner, Dick, Rick McHugh, and Dean Brumbaugh. *Rural Profile of Idaho.* Boise, Idaho: Idaho Division of Financial Management, 1990.

General Accounting Office. *Rural Development: Rural America Faces Many Challenges.* Washington, D.C.: GAO Report, 1992.

German Marshall Fund of the United States. *An Introductory Guide: Flexible Business Networks.* Washington, D.C.: German Marshall Fund, 1992.

Howard, Robert. "Can Small Business Help Countries Compete?" *Harvard Business Review* (November-December, 1990).

John, Patricia LaCaille. *Rural Entrepreneurship and Small Business Development*. Beltsville, Md.: Rural Information Center/National Agricultural Library, 1990.

Johnson, Dirk. "Small Towns Team Up to Fight Bleak Future" *New York Times*, 1 August 1992, A-1.

Johnson, Kirk. *Beyond Polarization: Emerging Strategies for Reconciling Community and the Environment*. Seattle: Northwest Policy Center, March 1993.

Joint Economic Committee. *Toward Rural Development Policy for the 1990's: Enhancing Income and Employment Opportunities*. Washington, D.C.: GPO, 1989.

Kemmis, Daniel. *Community and the Politics of Place*. Norman: University of Oklahoma Press, 1990.

Kennedy, Maureen, Robert A. Rapoza, Norman DeWeaver, and George Rucker. *Searching for the Way That Works: An Analysis of FmHA Rural Development Policy and Implementation*. Washington, D.C.: The Center for Community Change, 1990.

Kennedy, Paul. *Preparing for the Twenty-first Century*. New York: Random House, 1993.

Lawrence, Robert Z. *Can America Compete?* Washington, D.C.: The Brookings Institution, 1984.

Lustig, Nora, Barry P. Bosworth, and Robert Z. Lawrence, eds. *North American Free Trade: Assessing the Impact*. Washington, D.C.: The Brookings Institution, 1992.

Luther, Vicki, and Milan Wall. *The Entrepreneurial Community: A Strategic Planning Approach to Community Survival*. Lincoln, Nebr.: Heartland Center for Leadership Development, 1986.

Macke, Donald, Jerry Hoffman, and Marty Strange. *Neither Here Nor There: Quasi-Public Corporations and Economic Development in the Middle Border*. Walthill, Nebr.: Center for Rural Affairs, 1991.

Marshall, Ray, and Marc Tucker. *Thinking for a Living: Education and the Wealth of Nations. New York: Basic Books*, 1992.

Mayer, Neil S. *Neighborhood Organizations and Community Development: Making Revitalization Work*. Washington, D.C.: The Urban Institute, 1984.

MDC. *Coming Out of the Shadows: The Changing Face of Rural Development in the South*. Chapel Hill, N.C.: MDC, Inc., May 1992.

Muller, Brian. *Rural Economic Strategies and the State Development Budget: Issues and Policy, Options for the "New Texas."*. Austin: Texas Center for Policy Studies, 1992.

National Commission on Agriculture and Rural Development Policy. *Future Directions in Rural Development Policy*. Washington: National Commission on Agriculture and Rural Development Policy, 1990.

National Council for Urban Economic Development. *Competitive Advantage: Framing a Strategy to Support High Growth Firms*. Washington, D.C.: National Council for Urban Economic Development, 1984.

National Governors' Association. *New Alliances for Rural America: Report of the Task Force on Rural Development*. Washington, D.C.: National Governors' Association, 1988.

National Planning Association. *Positioning Agriculture for the 1990s: A New Decade of Change*. Washington, D.C.: National Planning Association, 1989.

North, Douglass C. *Institutions, Institutional Change and Economic Performance*. New York: Cambridge University Press, 1990.

Northwest Policy Center. *A Northwest Reader: Options for Rural Communities*. Seattle: University of Washington, Northwest Policy Center, 1989.

Northwest Policy Center. *Entrepreneurial Strategies: Readings on Flexible Manufacturing Networks*. Seattle: University of Washington, Northwest Policy Center 1992.

Olson, Mancur. *The Rise and Decline of Nations: Economic Growth, Stagflation, and Social Rigidities*. New Haven: Yale University Press, 1982.

Osborne, David. *Economic Competitiveness: The States Take the Lead*. Washington, D.C.: Economic Policy Institute, 1987.

Ospina, Enrique, and Cami S. Sims, eds. *The Role of State Government in Agriculture*. Morrilton, Ark.: Winrock International Institute for Agricultural Development, 1988.

Parker, Edwin B., Heather E. Hudson, Don A. Dillman, and Andrew D. Roscoe. *Rural America in the Information Age: Telecommunications Policy for Rural Development*. Lanham, Md.: University Press of America/Aspen Institute, 1989.

Peirce, Neal R., and Carol F. Steinbach. *Enterprising Communities: Community-Based Development in America*, 1990. Washington, D.C.: Council for Community-Based Development, 1990.

Pelton, Joseph N. "The Globalization of Universal Telecommunications Services." In *Universal Telephone Service: Ready for the 21st Century*. Queenstown, Md.: Institute for Information Studies/Aspen Institute/Northern Telecom, 1991.

Phillips, Phillip D. *Economic Development for Small Communities and Rural Areas*. Urbana-Champaign: University of Illinois, 1990.

Pink, Cheryl, Noreen Scott, and Laura Adams Dudley, eds. *Community Development Training Manual*. Amarillo, Tex.: Southwestern Public Service Company/New Mexico Economic Development Department, 1990.

Porter, Michael. *The Competitive Advantage of Nations*. New York: Basic Books, 1990.

President's Commission for a National Agenda for the Eighties. *Report*. Washington, D.C.: GPO, 1980.

Pulver, Glen C. *Community Economic Development Strategies*. Madison: University of Wisconsin-Extension, 1986.

Pulver, Glen, and David Dodson. *Designing Development Strategies in Small Towns*. Washington, D.C.: The Aspen Institute, 1992.

Radin, Beryl A. "Rural Development Councils: An Intergovernment Coordination Experiment" *Publius: The Journal of Federalism* 22, no. 3 (Summer 1992): 111-127.

Reed, B.J., and Robert Blair. "Economic Development in Rural Communities: Can Strategic Planning Make a Difference?" *Public Administration Review* 53, no.1, (January/February 1993): 88-92.

Report of the Commission on the Skills of the American Workforce. *America's Choice: high skills or low wages*. Rochester, N.Y.: National Center on Education and the Economy, June 1990.

Roberts, Brandon. *Competition Across the Atlantic: The States Face Europe '92*. Denver, Colo.: National Conference of State Legislatures, 1991.

Rosenfeld, Stuart with Philip Shapira and J. Trent Williams. *Smart Firms in Small Towns*. Washington, D.C.: Aspen Institute, 1992.

Rosenfeld, Stuart A. *Technology, Innovation and Rural Development*. Washington, D.C.: Aspen Institute, 1990.

Salant, Priscilla. *A Community Researcher's Guide to Rural Data*. Washington, D.C.: Island Press/ Aspen Institute, 1990.

Salant, Priscilla. *Community Development Organizations and Research: What Works and Why?* Washington, D.C.: The Aspen Institute, 1988.

Schuler, Galen, and Richard Gardner. "Pacific Northwest Strategy Community Development Guide," Working Draft. Prepared for USDA Forest Service Regions; Portland, Oregon, 1990.

Schwartz, Peter. *The Art of the Long View*. New York: Currency/Doubleday, 1991.

Senge, Peter M. *The Fifth Discipline: The Art & Practice of the Learning Organization*. New York: Currency/Doubleday, 1990.

Shepard, John C., Colleen Boggs Murphy, Louis D. Higgs, and Philip M. Burgess. *A New Vision of the Heartland: The Great Plains in Transition, Overview of Change in America's New Economy*. Denver, Colo.: Center for the New West, 1992.

Sherman, Arloc. *Falling by the Wayside: Children in Rural America*. Washington, D.C.: Children's Defense Fund, 1992.

Siegel, Beth, and Peter Kwass. *Aiding Rural Economies: A National Survey of Business Lending with State CDBG Funds*. Washington, D.C.: Council of State Community Affairs Agencies, 1990.

Sidor, John. *Put Up or Give Way: States, Economic Competitiveness, and Poverty*. Washington, D.C.: Council of State Community Development Agencies, 1991.

Sokolow, Alvin D., and Julie Spezia. *Political Leaders as Entrepreneurs? Economic Development in Small Communities*. Washington, D.C.: Economic Research Service, U.S. Department of Agriculture, October 1990.

Stegner, Wallace. *Beyond the Hundredth Meridian*. New York: Penguin Books, 1992.

Stern, Joyce D., ed. *The Condition of Education in Rural Schools*. Washington, D.C.: U.S. Department of Education, Office of Educational Research and Improvement, forthcoming.

Strange, Marty, Patricia E. Funk, Gerald Hansen, Jennifer Tully, and Donald Macke. *Half a Glass of Water: State Economic Development Policies and The Small Agricultural Communities of the Middle Border*. Walthill, Nebr.: Center for Rural Affairs, 1990.

Taub, Richard P. *Community Capitalism: Banking Strategies and Economic Development*. Boston: Harvard Business School Press, 1988.

Teater, Bonnie, ed. *National Rural Entrepreneurship Symposium*. Mississippi State University, Mississippi State: Southern Rural Development Center, 1987.

Thomas, Margaret G., Project Leader. *Recouple—Natural Resource Strategies for Rural Economic Development*. Kansas City, Mo.: Midwest Research Institute, 1990.

Tisdale, Jacqueline F., ed., *Guidebook for Rural Economic Development Training*. Mississippi State University, Mississippi State: Southern Rural Development Center, 1989.

Tyson, Laura D'Andrea. "They Are Not Us: Why American Ownership Still Matters" *The American Prospect* 4 (Winter 1991):37-53.

Unruh, Thomas, and Jay Kayne. *State-Federal Collaboration on Rural Development*. Economic Development and Commerce Policy Studies, Center for Policy Research. Washington, D.C.: National Governors' Association, 1992.

U.S. Department of Agriculture. *Financial Market Intervention As A Rural Development Strategy*. Washington, D.C.: Economic Research Service, December 1990.

U.S. Department of Agriculture. *Growth and Stability of Rural Economics in the 1980s: Differences Among Countries*. Staff Report prepared by David W. Sears, John M. Redman, Lorin D. Kusmin, and Molly S. Killian. Washington, D.C.: Economic Research Service, 1992.

U.S. Department of Agriculture. *Infrastructure Investment and Economic Development: Rural Strategies for the 1990s*. Washington, D.C.: Economic Research Service, December 1990.

U.S. Department of Agriculture. *Rural Economic Development in the 1980's: Prospects for the Future*. A special report prepared and edited by David L. Brown, J. Norman Reid, Herman Bluestone, David A. McGranahan, and Sara M. Mazie. Washington, D.C. Economic Research Service, 1988.

U.S. Department of Agriculture. *Tourism as a Rural Economic Development Tool: An Exploration of the Literature*. A special report prepared by Martha Frederick. Washington, D.C.: Economic Research Service, 1992.

Wall, Milan, and Vicki Luther. *Clues to Rural Community Survival*. Lincoln, Nebr.: Heartland Center for Leadership Development, 1987.

Walter, Susan, and Pat Choate. *Thinking Strategically: A Primer for Public Leaders*. Washington, D.C.: Council of State Planning Agencies, 1984.

Wilson, Robert H., and Paul E. Teske. "Telecommunications and Economic Development: The State and Local Role." *Economic Development Quarterly* 4 no.2 (May 1990): 158-174.

OTHER PUBLICATIONS BY CGPA

Scenarios of State Government in the Year 2010: Thinking about the Future, *Thomas W. Bonnett and Robert L. Olson*

New Alliances in Innovation: A Guide To Encouraging Innovative Applications of New Communication Technologies to Address State Problems, *Nancy Ginn Helme*

State and Local Tax Policy and the Telecommunications Industry, *Karl E. Case*

Managing the Policy Agenda: Organizational Options for Governors, *National Governors' Association and Council of Governors' Policy Advisors*

Experiments in Systems Change: States Implement Family Policy, *Judith K. Chynoweth, Lauren Cook, Michael D. Campbell and Barbara Dyer*

Improving Public Policy: States and Grantmakers Working Together, *Carolyn Cavicchio, Lauren Cook and John Riggan*

Getting Results: A Guide for Government Accountability, *Jack A. Brizius and Michael D. Campbell*

Strategic Policy for the Nation's Governors: Organizing for Effective Policy Development and Implementation, *Lauren Cook*, Ed.

State Technology Programs: A Preliminary Analysis of Lessons Learned, *David Osborne*

Thinking Strategically: A Primer for Public Leaders, *Susan Walter and Pat Choate*

The Game Plan: Governing with Foresight, *John D. Olsen and Douglas C. Eadie*

The Challenge of Telecommunications: State Regulatory and Tax Policies, *Karl E. Case and Charles Zielinski*

Renewing America: Natural Resource Assets and State Economic Development, *William E. Nothdurft*

The Safety Net as Ladder: Transfer Payments for Economic Development, *Robert E. Friedman*

On the Rebound: Helping Workers Cope with Plant Closings, *Terry F. Buss and Roger J. Vaughan*

Anticipating Tomorrow's Issues: A Handbook for Policymakers, *Lauren Cook, B. Jack Osterholt, and Edward C. Riley, Jr.*

ABOUT THE AUTHOR

Tom Bonnett's family has lived in Vermont for at least seven generations; both of Tom's grandfathers farmed in the Connecticut River Valley. He attended a one-room schoolhouse during part of first grade, second grade, and part of third grade. In 1974, he was elected to the Vermont House of Representatives from Thetford, Fairlee, West Fairlee, and Vershire. He served on the House Education Committee and was reelected in 1976.

He graduated from Bennington College in 1975 and received a master's degree from the University of California Graduate School of Public Policy at Berkeley in 1980. During the 1980s, he worked for a congressman, held several positions in New York City government, and ran a local, nonprofit development organization in Flushing, N.Y. He is currently the Director of Economic Development and Environment for the Council of Governors' Policy Advisors.

 Recycled Paper